UNDERSTANDING PANIC ATTACKS

AND OVERCOMING FEAR

DR ROGER BAKER

UNDERSTANDING PANIC ATTACKS

AND OVERCOMING FEAR

LION

A Lion Book
an imprint of
Lion Hudson plc
Wilkinson House, Jordan Hill Road,
Oxford OX2 8DR, England
www.lionhudson.com
ISBN 978 0 7459 5545 2

First edition 1995
This edition 2011
10 9 8 7 6 5 4 3 2 1 0

Distributed by:
UK: Marston Book Services, PO Box 269, Abingdon, Oxon, OX14 4YN
USA: Trafalgar Square Publishing, 814 N. Franklin Street, Chicago, IL 60610
USA Christian Market: Kregel Publications, PO Box 2607, Grand Rapids,
Michigan 49501

This book has been printed on paper and board independently certified
as having been produced from sustainable forests.

A catalogue record for this book is available
from the British Library

Typeset in 9/12 Arial (OTF) and 11/12 Bell MT
Printed and bound in the UK by CPI Cox & Wyman, Reading

CONTENTS

ACKNOWLEDGMENTS

I would like to thank all the patients who have allowed me to quote their experiences in this book. I am indebted to my wife, Ann, who painstakingly typed this manuscript on the basis of my indecipherable handwritten pages, and gave me really useful feedback on the balance and emphasis of the book. Lisa Gale, Dan Marshall, and Eimear Corrigan, research psychologists, read the second edition of the book, researched the latest developments in panic, and provided invaluable advice and recommendations on the shape of this new edition. Lastly, I would like to acknowledge the role of Malcolm McFadyen, a clinical psychologist with whom I worked at the Royal Cornhill Hospital in Aberdeen, and who originally developed the ideas behind the cognitive therapy approach described in this book.

1

PANIC: THE LIFE-CHANGING EVENT

"I would gladly have sold my soul to the devil for just one day of complete health. I would unhesitatingly have given away everything I had to anyone who could have guaranteed just twenty-four hours of normal health."

"I have been a sufferer for almost twenty-nine years, since I was serving with the Royal Navy. Of course, I don't have to tell you the hell that I have existed in."

"I see a man hobbling past my house on crutches, a cripple for life, and I actually envy him."

What are these people talking about? Why are they so desperate? What is it that is so bad that they would envy a man on crutches? The answer is panic anxiety.

We all know what anxiety is like – before an exam, when we have to give an important speech, reaching the finals in a sports event, or going to the dentist. But when anxiety breaks through into a person's life in a really powerful way and there seems to be no good reason for it, that is different. Daily life, work, and relationships can get more and more disrupted by these unpleasant feelings that cannot be controlled.

LIKE LIVING IN HELL

It can really begin to feel like living in hell as sufferers twist and turn, trying to shake off these feelings. People with panic anxiety often say that it is impossible for others to understand what they are going through, "like explaining the colour red to a blind person". The frustrating thing is that once they seemed to be leading an ordinary life. Then one day panic struck, and everything changed. Now they live in dread of unbearable panic feelings and wonder if they will ever get back to normal again.

Mrs A. went to the checkout at Morrisons to pay for some shopping and felt her heart starting to race and her mouth go dry. She couldn't get her money out of her purse because her hands were shaking so much. She rushed home. After this, she was overcome with anxiety every time she left the house alone. She had to be accompanied by one of her family. Even now, years later, she dreads going out of the house, and goes to great lengths to make sure she is never left in the house by herself.

Miss M. loved her job as a travel consultant, but after a panic attack on a busy train in Italy, she gave up work altogether, and after a long spell she was only prepared to work in a rather undemanding job involving no travel.

Mr P. would start to shake and tremble and feel nauseous during meetings at his work in the oil industry. He was sure he would vomit or be seen shaking by his colleagues, and had made so many excuses for leaving meetings that he felt his job was in jeopardy.

Mrs C. dearly wanted children but because of panic attacks put it off and off until it was too late. "I thought, 'How could I cope with a baby?... So often I'm housebound.'"

These are descriptions of people who have had panic attacks. No two people describe it in quite the same way. For some, it is the heart palpitations that are unbearable, for others dizzy sensations or feeling unreal, and for others difficulty in breathing or choking sensations. But they all share one thing. Their lives have been devastated by panic anxiety. One attack on a fateful day turned their life around and took it in a direction they did not want or choose. It made them look inwards at themselves rather than outwards. It put a strain on their relationships. It was a daily source of dread.

WHAT IS A PANIC ATTACK?

Throughout the centuries people have suffered from panic attacks. In sixteenth-century France, they called them *terreur panique*. One English writer described panic attacks in 1603 as "sudden foolish frights, without any certeine cause, which they call panique terrores". Sigmund Freud was one of the first to give an accurate description of panic attacks in 1884, calling them "anxiety attacks" rather than panic attacks. Panic attacks were fairly much ignored by the medical and psychological professions until a century later. In 1980, the American Psychiatric Association included "panic attacks" in their *Diagnostic and Statistical Manual*, a sort of psychiatrist's Bible for diagnosing emotional problems. The definition in this manual has become the accepted standard of what a panic attack is. The updated manual of 2000[1] states that the following thirteen sensations are the main ones to occur in panic attacks:

- palpitations, pounding heart, or accelerated heart rate

- sweating

- trembling or shaking

- shortness of breath or smothering sensations

- feeling of choking

- chest pain or discomfort

- feeling nauseous or having a nervous tummy

- dizziness, unsteadiness, or faintness

- feeling unreal or "depersonalized" (feeling detached from oneself)

- fear of loss of control or going crazy

- fear of dying

11

- numbness or tingling feelings
- chills or hot flushes.

To qualify as a panic attack, four of these feelings (any four) have to start suddenly, unexpectedly, and reach a peak within a ten-minute period. There should be no obvious life-threatening situation setting them off.

Many sufferers experience more than four sensations. The sort of sensations they notice may not be exactly the same one week as another week. What bothers one person may not bother another. The term "limited panic attacks" is used when someone suffers from only one or two of these feelings out of the blue. I am saying "only" one or two, but this gives the wrong impression, because for these people one or two of these sensations catching them unawares can be worrying, aggravating, and frequent enough to spoil their lives.

CAN I BE NORMAL IF I HAVE PANIC ATTACKS?

Although the *Diagnostic and Statistical Manual* has been very useful in drawing attention to panic attacks, it has been unhelpful in another way. The manual invented the term "panic *disorder*" for people who regularly have panic attacks or live in fear of panic. While it may be useful to have a medical-sounding name for insurance claims, it unfortunately gives the impression that the person is suffering from some sort of medical illness or disease, which panic is not.

Panic attacks can be explained by normal psychological processes occurring in a normal mind. They can be explained with reference to the unhealthy way people have learned to cope with life's stresses, their lack of knowledge and misunderstanding of what is going on in their bodies, and their *fear* of what might happen to them. Fear, lack of knowledge, and misunderstanding are common to all humanity and have nothing to do with illness.

CAN FEAR AND PANIC BE OVERCOME?

Many sufferers have looked for help from different quarters. Some go to their own doctor and are helped by the drugs they have been prescribed. Some get referred on to specialist cardiologists or neurologists, believing that they are suffering from a physical disease, and are left confused when nothing is found. Others seek the advice of friends, go for counselling, or turn to the clergy. Some find their way to short-term relief by using alcohol. Some scrape along – somehow coping but never living life to the full. For others, nothing seems to work – it is like living in a nightmare.

But is it possible to change? Can the feelings disappear? Can life be normal again? The answer is yes, it is possible to change – not overnight, but it is possible. This book is written to help people through the maze of panic symptoms and to emerge at the other side free from their domination. It is certainly not easy, or quick, but it definitely is possible.

WHO IS THIS BOOK WRITTEN FOR?

It is written for three groups of people.

- It is a self-help guide for panic sufferers; this is its main purpose.[2]

- It is intended to help relatives, partners, and friends of panic sufferers to understand their problems and to provide informed help to the sufferer. Usually these people suffer too, because the problem is so baffling and they are never sure of the right way to react to the sufferer. Should they be firm, sympathetic, or what? Is it illness or weakness, or is the sufferer overreacting?

- It is also designed for therapists to use alongside their therapy sessions. For about four years before publication of the first edition, I gave clients early versions of Chapters 4 to 8 to read between sessions. It can help in backing up what the therapist has said. Clients often find that written material helps them in digesting the information and adds to the therapy.

Therapists vary greatly in the approach they take to problems. Although this book is primarily cognitive behavioural in orientation, I have tried to bear this in mind – different therapists will find that different sections in the book complement their own approach. In this case, they need only direct their clients to the sections they feel are relevant.

CAN PEOPLE HELP THEMSELVES?

One of the worst problems about panic and anxiety is not knowing what is happening. I have called this book *Understanding Panic Attacks and Overcoming Fear* because I am convinced that understanding is one of the main keys to unlocking recovery.

■ UNDERSTANDING

I have seen many clients in therapy whose panic attacks have faded after one session of explanation about what they really are and what they are not. Knowledge about what is happening to them brings reassurance and hope in place of bewilderment. Part I provides some basic information about panic. Part II explains what is actually happening during panic and deals with common misunderstandings.

Another important part of understanding is in a personal sense – why did this happen to me? Part III of this book is devoted to understanding causes of panic; it looks at these causes in two senses. First, stressful life events in the panic sufferer's life, and second, how these have built up to panic proportions. This third part explains "emotional processing" – that is, the way in which the body neutralizes or absorbs emotional hurt, making it a type of natural healing process.

Part IV of the book describes a programme of practical therapy exercises to overcome the fear of panic. This is a psychological treatment programme that was originally devised by psychologist Malcolm McFadyen in the late 1970s and used at the Department of Clinical Psychology in Aberdeen,

Scotland, to treat hundreds of anxiety sufferers successfully.[3] The technical name for the approach is "Cognitive Invalidation", and it is based on the pioneering work of Isaac Marks in developing behavioural exposure at the Institute of Psychiatry, King's College, London,[4] combined with the cognitive theories of George Kelly.[5] I worked closely with Malcolm for fifteen years in developing the approach. It is a close relative to Aaron Beck and David Clark's cognitive therapy for panic,[6] as well as David Barlow's "Panic Control Therapy".[7] Cognitive therapies have been extensively researched and shown in controlled scientific trials to be effective with panic attacks. They are practised worldwide by clinical psychologists and cognitive therapists. Many sufferers find that if they know the right approach they can go ahead and make progress fast.

■ WITH A LITTLE HELP FROM MY FRIENDS
I would advise anyone intending to use Part IV of the book (Practical Therapy Exercises) to have a friend or partner to back them up. The helper should also read the earlier parts of the book. This will help them to understand what the problem and the treatment are about, so that they can support and help the sufferer, who may feel like giving up or become impatient with their lack of progress (this nearly always happens).

■ PROFESSIONAL HELP
Some sufferers, despite having a friend to support them, need a bit more professional help than this. They may need to contact a clinical psychologist, cognitive-behavioural therapist, or local self-help group to help them recover. In the "Help for Panic Sufferers" section (see page 170), there are some useful websites, reading material, and a helpline for sufferers to consult.

■ USE OF DRUGS
The therapy programme in this book does not depend on using medicines or drug prescriptions. It does not mean that sufferers should stop using any drugs they are prescribed, but that if they want, people using this book can overcome panic without

drugs. Some people are against using drugs because they would prefer to be in control, even though this involves some suffering. Others prefer to take something that may help to reduce their suffering.

This decision is completely up to sufferers. They should not feel guilty if taking drugs; on the other hand they should not feel that the *only* way to recover is through using drugs. It is a matter of personal preference.

Lastly, Part V, called "The Panic Sufferer as Normal", explains in more detail how panic follows rational and reasonable psychological rules. It is the product of a normal mind, not a deranged one.

WHERE DO THE IDEAS IN THIS BOOK COME FROM?

The information and ideas in this book come from eight different sources:

- Personal experience in treating panic-attack sufferers over a thirty-two-year period in the UK National Health Service and in private therapy.

- Reading research documents on panic and communicating with leading authorities (such as Isaac Marks and David Barlow) as part of compiling a book called *Panic Disorder: Theory, Research and Therapy*, published in 1989.[8]

- Study of autobiographies and published case histories on agoraphobia and panic.[9]

- A research interview study carried out on twenty panic sufferers in 1990. Interviews were tape-recorded and transcribed. Most of the quotes in this book are taken from these interviews.

- The development in the theoretical understanding of cognitive therapy and panic at the Department of Psychology, Aberdeen, from 1977 to 1993.[10]

- Research information gathered on 130 panic and anxiety patients, 177 medically ill, and 521 ordinary members of the public. Information was gathered on the last two groups to compare with panic sufferers.[11]

- An evaluation study carried out on every patient seen for therapy at the Psychology department, Aberdeen, between 1991 and 1993, including every panic sufferer seen during that time.

- Research into how emotional processing style can enhance the healing process and reduce anxiety.[12]

THE PROOF OF THE PUDDING...

Julio Sánchez-Meca and colleagues at the Psychology department, University of Murcia, Spain, carried out a full-scale search of all scientifically controlled studies of cognitive therapy for panic sufferers.[13] In all, they looked at sixty-five research studies from around the world, which in total evaluated the therapy of about 2,500 patients. They assessed all the different varieties of cognitive therapy to find out which was the best. This could be likened to comparing different hybrid strains of the same plant. While most of the "varieties" were successful, the single most effective approach was "exposure", which is the foundation stone of the approach described in this book. They found the approach was equally successful with males and females of any age, and whether or not they were taking medication.

Although the Sánchez-Meca review and National Institute of Clinical Excellence (NICE)[14] guidelines on panic in 2004 provide strong evidence for exposure-based cognitive therapy, the Department of Psychology at Aberdeen also conducted their own naturalistic study of cognitive invalidation therapy.

Every panic patient referred to the Clinical Psychology department for therapy by a doctor or psychiatrist between 1991 and 1993 was assessed. Patients filled in self-report questionnaires on their problems before they started therapy,

Figure 1: Panic attack sufferers; improvement during therapy

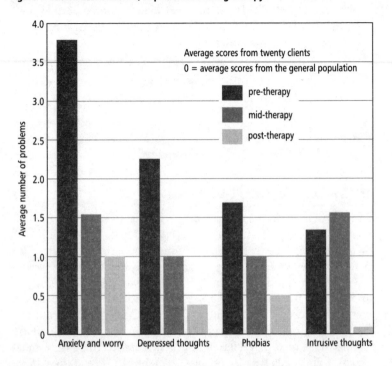

three months after therapy had begun, and after six months, which was towards the end of therapy. Other patients on the waiting list who had not yet received any therapy filled in the same questionnaire over six months to act as a comparison for the panic group in therapy.

Figure 1 (above) shows how much panic sufferers changed during the course of therapy. The figure shows how many problems/symptoms the patients reported before, during, and after therapy, divided into four main "symptom areas". The zero point is based on the scores of a large sample of local people; this helps us to see how close to "normal" panic sufferers can get after therapy. As you can see, patients improved during therapy in every symptom area. The patients on the waiting list showed no change during this time. The difference between the two groups was statistically significant. This indicates that the use of the Cognitive Invalidation approach significantly helped to reduce anxiety, fear, depression, and intrusive thoughts for these panic sufferers. Notice with intrusive thoughts that there is a slight deterioration at mid-therapy before improvement at post-therapy. This is probably because the therapy programme involves facing fear, which temporarily increases disturbing thoughts before the benefits kick in. By the end of therapy, their scores were very close to scores from the sample of healthy local people.[15]

This suggests that this cognitive approach was successful when used by clinical psychologists. What this book aims to do is to make the same approach available to readers, and provide an extra resource to therapists as they treat panic sufferers.

PART I

THE A TO Z OF PANIC

2

PANIC:
WHEN AND WHERE

Panic attacks or anxiety attacks first occur "out of the blue", suddenly, for no obvious reason. A person may have been living much as anyone else does with the usual stresses and strains of life when one day they experience a panic attack that is the start of a long period of misery and change. The peak time for first attacks is between the ages of fifteen and thirty, although attacks can occur at any age.

It has been estimated that one in ten people experience panic attacks,[1] but only 1–3.5 per cent of the population experience panic problems so severe that they seriously interfere with their life. I have often asked people what they themselves call these attacks. Often they give it the name panic without having heard of it from anyone else. Some people think of it as a nervous breakdown – "I had a breakdown" – and they feel they cannot carry on at work or have the same active life. Sometimes people give up promising careers.

OUT OF A CLEAR BLUE SKY

The worrying thing about a first attack is that it comes without warning and sufferers can see no good reason why such a dramatic thing should happen to them – though as I will show later there is always a cause. What can really confuse people is that the first panic attack can strike when they least expect it – during a relaxing weekend or on holiday. They might understand it better if it struck while they were under a lot of stress at home or work, but not when it seems unconnected to stress.

After the first panic attack, more attacks can happen over the next few days and weeks so that they become a regular feature of life. There are seven common patterns of panic.

1. PLACE

Some people find panics occur in certain places, such as crowded shops, travelling on a bus, standing in a queue, in church, being in a city centre. The name agoraphobia, from the Greek "fear (*phobos*) of the marketplace (*agora*)", has been used in the past for this type of panic. For these people, "safety" is also a place, usually home, where they begin to feel secure and relieved. They may try to avoid crowds and shops, sometimes to the extent of becoming completely housebound. Here are two examples:

"It was a Sunday. I went into the bingo, and I couldna concentrate. My hands started shaking. I tried to mark the number off the card. I couldna do it, and I telt mysel, 'Dinna be sae stupid.' I couldna see the number, you know, and my hands started shakin' and everything, and I felt ma body… yer stomach was rumbling… and my neck started to twitch, and I says me, 'I'm nae going back to bingo,' 'cause I felt some people was looking at me."
Ann P.

"I began to have attacks in crowded places – particularly the student union at weekends. The predominant feeling then was that I could not breathe, although my heart would also be racing. When this happened, I would generally leave and find somewhere to sit and recover… Later I would also panic in lectures… I had a few attacks when outside; usually in hot, stuffy and disorientatingly large shops or when I had to stand around waiting for someone."
Jane S-T.

2. SITUATION

Some people panic because of the situation they are put in. Some panic if they find themselves trapped in a room where they cannot see the exit. For them, safety means knowing where an "escape route" is, in case the panic starts. Others panic if trapped for a period of time such as having a doctor's or dentist's appointment. For these people, safety means avoiding these situations, or trying not to commit themselves to things. Some panic if they have to carry out stressful things alone. For them, safety means only doing things with a partner, trusted friend, or relative. Here are a few illustrations:

■ TRAPPED IN A ROOM
"As a newspaper reporter I found the problems of attending crowded council meetings in stuffy committee rooms with no easy avenue of escape to be quite overwhelming, particularly when I had to leave the room for a fourth or fifth time to attend to the needs of acute panic (going to the toilet)."
Ruth Hurst Vose, from her book *Agoraphobia*[2]

■ TRAPPED FOR A FIXED TIME
"When I was in an exam on 12 March, my hands went shaky; I broke out in a cold sweat and felt physically sick. I felt I'd go out of control and worried I'd start screaming. I had a panic feeling… a feeling like running."
Ron H.

■ BEING ALONE
"If there's nobody in the house, or my husband's not speaking to me, or anything like that, my body starts panicking and I feel like saying to myself, 'Well, I'll disappear'… I feel like disappearing… getting away you know. I just feel like running away."
Penny G.

3. FEELINGS

What sets a panic attack off for many sufferers is experiencing feelings in their body. This may include feeling hot, sweating, heart beating faster, and dizzy feelings. Often these feelings are set off by quite normal events, though sufferers do not realize this at the time. They may sweat because the room is hotter, or their hearts may beat faster because they are walking, or they may feel dizzy because they are hungry. Other sensations that may worry them are going from dark to light places, higher atmospheric pressure, neon lighting, the surface and texture of floors, or feelings of fullness after a meal.

Having the flu very often sets off panic because the feelings – light-headedness, sweatiness, and fever – resemble a panic attack very closely; usually sufferers do not recognize that it is simply the flu. For some, *any* change in bodily sensations is enough to set off panic. One man I saw for therapy had given up cigarettes, never took alcohol and refused to take any medication for his very severe panic. He said:

"I'm scared of drugs. I hate having an induced feeling put on me. I panic as soon as I get a feeling that's not happening naturally. If it comes from alcohol, I would panic even if the feelings are positive ones. I stopped the cigarettes for one reason (health), but for another really – fear."
John S.

For these people, safety means trying to avoid having the feelings they fear. This may mean always keeping cool, trying to avoid sweating by keeping the windows open (very annoying for the rest of the family), trying to stop raised heart rate by walking slowly upstairs and avoiding "bloated feelings" by never eating large meals. It generally means that they have to be very careful not to set off certain feelings. They may also take medication to reduce feelings, such as beta blockers, which slow down heart rate. If they are unsuccessful in their attempts to avoid having feelings, they also have up their sleeves things they can do to neutralize the unwanted feelings. These include lying very still, going out into the cool fresh air, relaxation, and taking bicarbonate.

4. ANTICIPATION

Some panic sufferers experience panic before they have to do something difficult, in the build-up period. Many find a planned holiday excruciating as the time for departure approaches. The anxiety in waiting is usually worse than the event itself but by the time they get to the event they have exhausted themselves so much they have little strength to deal with the panic. For these people, avoidance means never committing themselves to doing things but going on the spur of the moment. If they feel an attack coming on, they may cancel even quite expensive events, such as holidays, and become embarrassed about having to lie or make excuses to others for opting out.

"The unpleasant symptoms of fear, which I thought to be symptoms of illness, would strike whenever I ventured out, because I had been conditioned like the famous Pavlov's dogs, to expecting them to occur. In fact, sometimes the symptoms would be provoked simply by the knowledge that I had to leave the house."
Pauline McKinnon, from *In Stillness Conquer Fear*[3]

"We were going out for an Indian meal. It was a hen night. I was getting ready to go out when it started. The thought of rushing about."
Pauline L.

5. ACTIONS/LACK OF ACTIONS

The fifth main pattern of panic is to do with things the person does or does not do. Panic attacks may occur as the person watches television, relaxes, hears an argument, runs up the stairs, or has sexual intercourse. For these people, "safety" is doing something to help, such as lying down, running on the spot, sitting down, tensing up, deep breathing. It may also mean not doing certain things such as purposely not relaxing, not watching certain things on television, not reading certain things in the newspapers, not talking about or listening to some topics such as mental illness or heart attacks.

27

■ WATCHING TELEVISION

"I was sitting watching TV. I could feel it coming on. I had to get up and iron some clothes. It was getting worse – pain shooting through me... this can happen when people talk about heart attacks.

"My husband has to warn my friends not to talk about it. I'm frightened to pick up the paper... Sometimes I'm all at peace watching a film on TV when it comes on you."
Zena N.

"If I've had a lot to drink the night before, I have a lot of little panics the next day. Once when it was my last night on the (oil) rigs I was sitting watching a film on the rig when it suddenly came on."
James R.

■ HASSLES OR UPSETS

Robert Freedman, Director of the Behavioral Medicine Laboratory at Detroit,[4] reported a study in which panic sufferers noted their panic and anxiety while being "wired" for twenty-four-hour monitoring of heart rate, and temperature. He records:

Patient J. M. had spent the day at home resting, watching television and doing minor chores. She reported anxiety ratings of 20 [out of 100] throughout the day. Shortly after 8 p.m. her daughter came home from school and told her that another girl in school had threatened to kill her. J. M. became very upset about this, and at 8.15 p.m., she indicated she was having a panic attack [scoring 80 out of 100].

■ ARGUMENTS

W. T. had just had a telephone conversation with his partner with whom he had been arguing. This occurred just after he had begun the Medilog recording. At 10.25 a.m., he pressed the event marker to indicate a panic attack. He reported an anxiety rating of 60 [out of 100] and stated that the attack was caused by thinking about his conversation with his partner.

6. THOUGHTS ABOUT PANIC

For some people, just thinking about panic, hearing about it, or reading about it is enough to give them a panic attack. It is rather difficult to avoid thinking certain thoughts but people do attempt to avoid this by trying to distract their minds, filling their minds with activity, and never allowing themselves to relax or do nothing.

Here is an example taken from a therapist's session of a woman who panicked just because the subject of panic feelings was being discussed and it made her think about it.

Therapist: *Now you've got to accept your ability to feel anything.*
Patient: *Right.*
Therapist: *But the feelings are not…*
Patient: *Dr Zane, I think I'm going to have to go out for a minute or two.*
Therapist: *Now wait a minute, you can go out if you want to, but please explain to me what's happening.*
Patient: *Suddenly that wave of fear coming over me… it just makes me relive the panic attack and I fear it's coming on again. My mind slipped away from what you were saying and I was kind of focusing again on the two panic attacks I've had recently and that kind of feeling came over me.*
From M. D. Zane[5]

7. SLEEP

The seventh type of panic is connected with sleep. Some people are aware of fast heartbeats, sudden feelings of falling or jolting, or frightening feelings of unconsciousness as they drop off. Others awake bathed in sweat, or with a jolt, heart pounding. Some wake up struggling to breathe. Others wake up feeling they are paralysed (it seems that they are like this for ages, though it does not last long).

People with this type of panic may try to avoid certain things related to sleep, such as the sensation of dropping off to sleep.

Safety means trying to avoid falling asleep, waiting until it is light or sleeping half sitting up. Many do allow themselves to go to sleep, but to reduce "danger" they always ensure that they have someone to sleep next to them, or pills or a phone at hand "just in case". Sleeping tablets, alcohol or milky drinks may also be used just before bed to try to reduce unpleasant feelings.

"Panics initially occurred only at night, as I was falling asleep. It felt as if the bed was shaking rapidly and for some few weeks I wondered whether something could in fact be causing this – a neighbour's washing machine or a heavy lorry on the road outside. Having decided that this was unlikely and realizing that I was actually shaking I began to wonder whether there was some identifiable cause – was I drinking too much coffee or spending too long crouched over my computer? These explanations did not stand up to closer examination and I then began to consider whether there was something physically wrong with me.

"Around this time, certainly not much earlier, I began to anticipate that the panics would occur. They also became much more severe – they would still start with the feeling that the bed was shaking, but I would also become aware of my heartbeat and breathing. Following this warning, there would be a feeling as if something had dropped inside my chest – like a change of gear – and my heart would start pounding, I would feel as if I couldn't get a proper breath, feel dizzy and break out in sweat. On some occasions, I was woken up by this, and was convinced that this was because my breathing had been erratic, and that if I hadn't woken up I would have died.

"There were several nights when I was still awake and panicking at four or five in the morning, having had two or three attacks, each coming as I was just dropping off to sleep. The attacks varied in how long they lasted, from ten minutes to about half an hour – but it often took me a good hour after this to pluck up the courage to try to sleep again. I am certain that if sleep was not necessary, I would have avoided it altogether."
Jane S-T.

"It's a scary feeling because... well... I think it was last week I was... I was in my bed and I woke up with a start and couldn't feel my... I felt I was choking... I couldn't feel my body... you know... I seemed to have stiffened up."
Wilma W.

Although I have talked about seven main types of panic there is overlap between them, and most sufferers experience more than one kind.

PHOBIAS

Phobias, or irrational fears, are very common. There are many different types of phobia, including fear of insects, animals, heights, water, vomiting, blood, injections, hospitals, dentists, or meeting and having to talk to other people. For people with phobias, encountering the thing they fear brings on panic pretty much like clockwork. The problem is quite specific and quite predictable – sufferers are reasonably calm at other times but panic once they are near the thing they fear.

The sort of problem discussed in this book mainly involves panic attacks that occur more unpredictably – there seems to be no one obvious object that sets them off. Some psychologists have described panic as a "portable phobia". It is not "out there" like spiders, dogs, or bridges; the feared objects are feelings and sensations inside the person.

A survey of young people carried out in 2007 showed that 49 per cent had a mild phobia and 9 per cent a severe phobia that interfered with their lives.[6] Severely phobic persons are usually not only afraid of the object of fear itself – for example, spiders – but also frightened by the panic and how it might harm them. This book still has something to offer to people with such phobias, though it was written mainly for those struggling with unexplained panic and anxiety. And some unhappy people suffer with unexpected panic attacks *and* have severe specific phobias too. Life's not fair, is it?

3

HOW PANIC
CHANGES PEOPLE

Have you ever seen television pictures of a coastal town after it has been struck by a hurricane? The force of the wind and waves hits it full on, smashing trees and houses, ruining roads, and scattering debris all over the place. After the wind and sea have calmed down, dealing with the destruction and havoc in the town takes months. The hurricane may last one day, but the effects last much longer.

DEVASTATION

Panic is rather like that. Even after the original panics have struck, the sufferer reacts and reacts for a long time after. Let's look at the typical reactions that follow panic attacks.

■ STEP 1: FEAR STEPS IN
First, the sufferer becomes very afraid of having another attack, and very afraid of what *might* happen during the next attack. A sense of fear, dread, of impending doom creeps over them. For some, it may take two or three attacks before they are really scared; for others just one attack. Whereas their life before was normal enough, with its ups and downs, now fear spoils everything and takes away the joy from those little things that formerly gave them pleasure.

■ STEP 2: THE INNER FOCUS
Secondly, the sufferer develops an inner focus, shifting their attention away from what is going on around them and beginning to look inwardly. They do not concentrate properly on what others are saying, or the things they are doing, but are

too aware of their own feelings. It is as if their gaze was taken off the outside world and focuses on what is happening inside them.

Sufferers begin to notice feelings, sensations, pains – any changes in what is going on in the body. They become "body conscious". They begin to notice whether their heart is beating faster and may check their pulse. They notice if they are sweating more, breathing faster, feeling sick. They check to see if everything is working OK in the body – like a car in for its annual service – but this isn't an annual check, it's every five minutes! They are very aware of any sensations that feel like panic. They are so scared of panic happening again that they notice even slight feelings that may have occurred in panic.

The trouble with looking inwards is that our bodies are changing all the time. For instance, when we exert effort – walk or run – our heart will beat faster when we stop, quite naturally. But someone who is constantly checking and worrying about bodily changes may especially notice this. People can become "sensitized" or over-aware of just one or a whole range of feelings.

The net result of this inner focus is that people:

• unconsciously look out for the feelings they most dislike

• are very sensitive to even small amounts of the feeling

• are instantly aware of the feelings

• keep concentrating on the feelings once they happen.

■ STEP 3: FEAR OF FEELINGS
Thirdly, sufferers become afraid of certain feelings. If they think a panic attack was actually a heart attack, the feelings they are most afraid of may be increased heart rate, chest pain, sweating, or palpitations. If sufferers notice one of these feelings, they may start to be afraid.

One man I saw when I first began treating panic problems was very afraid of chest pains. He believed the "heart attack" would happen soon after he felt these pains. I asked him to keep an hourly diary of these chest pains over the following week. He came back the next week looking much happier. He had kept a diary and made little graphs of the strength of chest pains at different times during the day. He noticed these pains occurred twenty minutes after drinking coffee or eating a big meal and realized they were indigestion, not an impending heart attack!

People can also become afraid of certain thoughts as well as feelings. For instance, they may think, "I'm going mad," and become really scared of that thought running through their minds.

■ STEP 4: THE VICIOUS CIRCLE
Fourthly – and this is one of the keys to why panic attacks can continue to occur repeatedly – sufferers get into a vicious circle (see Figure 2, below). They may notice changes in their bodies, such as an increased heart rate. If they are afraid that a panic might start, the fear of this can create more feelings: the heart may start beating faster still, which makes them more afraid, which causes the heart to beat even faster. Their fear of panic may actually create a new panic attack. This has been noticed by many writers on anxiety. It has been called "fear of fear", "fear of bodily sensations", "negative spiral", and "negative feedback loop". Even a thought such as "I might have a panic" may be enough in one person to start this fear cycle going.

Figure 2: The vicious circle of panic

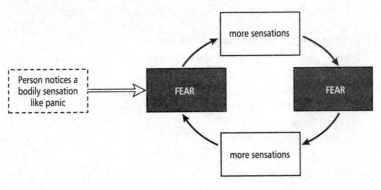

STEP 5: AVOIDANCE

Fifthly, sufferers' fears begin to change their lifestyle. They may start to avoid places or situations in which they have had a panic attack before, or where they reckon they might panic. Alternatively they may try to avoid doing or thinking things that might bring on panic. Figure 3 (below) illustrates this.

Figure 3: Avoidance patterns

FEAR OF PANIC	⇨ Avoidance of anything that the person *thinks* might set off a panic	⇨ Places	– avoid supermarkets, buses
		⇨ Situations	– avoid being alone, trapped situations
		⇨ Feelings	– walk slowly to avoid raising heartbeat
		⇨ Anticipation	– make no fixed plans to anxiously wait for future events
		⇨ Thoughts	– try to keep mind occupied to avoid thinking about panic
		⇨ Actions	– avoid arguments, watching TV
		⇨ Sleep	– sleep sitting up to avoid waking up with choking feelings

There are different levels of trying to avoid what they fear. These are:

Avoid altogether

This is the most straightforward approach, but it is the most devastating. One very sad description of this is *The Autobiography of David*.[1] It is the story of a famous journalist and writer whose panic and agoraphobia eventually left him completely housebound.

Try not to let a panic start ("safety routines")

There are many things that people do to ward off a panic before it strikes. Here are some typical safety routines:

• taking pills or alcohol before doing something difficult

- taking a trusted friend with them
- keep talking to someone on their mobile phone
- holding the hand of a child
- taking a dog or walking stick with them
- chewing peppermints
- holding themselves tense all the time
- wearing sunglasses
- keeping their mind occupied with other things at all times
- staying close to walls or near to doors
- only tackling things on "good days"
- trying to psych themselves up with "You'll be all right, you'll be all right".

Some therapists call these "talismans": as long as the person wears a "magical" token, or does a "magical" act, they believe they will be safe from harm. People develop hundreds of habits to prevent or avoid panic. One sufferer put it like this:

"Going shopping bears all the resemblance to planning a train robbery. Lines of escape must be worked out all the way, and as long as 'rabbit runs' exist on any outing, it can usually be tolerated."
Ruth Hurst Vose, from her book *Agoraphobia*[2]

Be prepared for the worst ("lifesavers")
This is the equivalent of always carrying around a first-aid kit in case disaster strikes. People can develop all sorts of tricks to bring feelings down to a manageable level once they start. Sometimes they take an object – a quarter-bottle of gin in the handbag, smelling salts, a self-help panic leaflet, and definitely their mobile phone so they can call for help.

Many sufferers keep a few tranquillizers in their purse or pocket "just in case" panic starts. These are often as much a psychological comfort as a real benefit. One man whom I saw as a patient felt fine when he had to attend a business convention – no anxiety, no panic – until he remembered he had forgotten his "safety" tranquillizer. Then his panic started. Many sufferers have developed their own list of things they can do, that they think will reduce panic once it starts. The list is endless: among other things, they may lie down on the bed, take a deep breath, drink water, drink alcohol, take Valium or some other tranquillizer, try to talk themselves out of it, open a window, go in or out of the house, run, or try to pretend they are not feeling sensations.

AVOIDANCE: LIVE NOW, PAY LATER

Although it may seem the natural thing to try to avoid, prevent or reduce panic it is only a short-term solution. It brings some relief *now*, but in the long run it only keeps the problem going. The person may think they are pouring water on the fire to put it out, but they have got hold of the wrong can and are pouring petrol on it instead. It is damaging to try to avoid having panic attacks because:

* it clutters up the sufferer's life to an incredible degree, narrowing their prospects and generally reducing the quality of their life;

* it means that if a panic does occur they are unprepared for it and have not learned how to cope;

* it keeps the sufferer from discovering the real truth: what would happen if they made no attempt to avoid, stop or minimize panic.

What *would* happen if the person did not try to fight panic at all? This may be a scary idea but, as following chapters show, it is one of the keys to successful therapy.

4

WHAT IS A PANIC ATTACK?

The human body is an amazing thing. Our bodies seem to be specially designed to save us and help us deal with harm. Take a cut on the finger – why doesn't the blood keep pouring out until we are dead? The body recognizes there is a cut and things change. When the blood comes into contact with the air, it reacts differently and starts to clot. The blood gets thicker and thicker and eventually forms a scab. After a few days, even that drops off and the whole thing is healed up. It works like clockwork; it doesn't matter if we are asleep or awake, unintelligent or a genius – the body heals up just the same. Automatically.

What happens if food or drink accidentally "goes down the wrong way", into the windpipe? We automatically cough and splutter. What does this do? It shoots the food or drink out of the windpipe at great speed. We keep on coughing until the unwanted food is safely out of our windpipe. We don't have to stop and think "Food in the windpipe is dangerous to the lungs – I must expel it"; the body automatically takes over and does the right thing – cough.

What if we eat some food that's going bad or is poisonous? The stomach automatically detects that something is wrong and shoots the food back up again – we are sick, we vomit – it is not pleasant but it does the trick, and the food is out of our system.

When we catch an illness such as the flu, viruses are detected in the body and special cells, antibodies, are produced to surround the viruses and "smother" them. Each time we get a new illness, new antibodies are created to deal with that particular virus next time, so that we develop our own personal databank of protection. The way in which antibodies work is so complicated it has taken researchers years to discover and there is still more to find out.

Yet the smallest child can produce antibodies without thinking. Our bodies are working day and night for our protection. The amazing thing is that it is all automatic.

I have used just four examples of how the body automatically looks after us. But there are thousands of ways it is trying to protect us. A hundred high spec computers could not look after us as cleverly as our bodies can. In this chapter I will be describing panic and anxiety symptoms, but as I do, I want us to keep firmly in mind that the body is an amazing protective machine, working for us even when things go wrong.

THE FEAR REACTION

One automatic type of protection in the body is the fear reaction. Let's say we are walking down a narrow alleyway when suddenly two snarling Rottweilers leap out at us, barking, with teeth flashing and saliva running down their jaws. Do we reason out: "This is a dog. It is snarling. It is biting my hand. I am in danger. I should take effective action. What should I do? Yes, I think running is the best solution"? No, not at all! We'd probably be mauled to death before we finished the thought process. No, what happens is that our body automatically reacts ultra-quickly. Adrenalin is pumped into the bloodstream; our heart pounds, we break out in a sweat and before we have time to think – in an instant – we are either fleeing like the wind or fighting the dogs off like a demon. This is the fear reaction. It is there to save us from harm.

We run like the wind away from the dogs. They are right behind us snapping and snarling but we move pretty quickly and get away. When we have run about 100 metres and reckon it is safe enough to stop, we turn round to see if they have stopped chasing us. What do we notice about our body?

- Our heart is beating like a train engine. Fast and hard.

- Our breathing is fast and deep.

- We are trembling and shaking and sweating all over.

- Our mouth is as dry as a bone.
- We feel a bit sick and dizzy.
- Our hands and feet are tingling.
- We are really very aroused, tense and alert, watching out for new danger.

Are we afraid? Well, we *were* afraid of the dogs, but now they seem to have settled down and are barking in the distance. We are not the least bit afraid of these changes in our body – even though there are many changes and the feelings are very strong. The feelings themselves do not bother us because we know exactly why we are feeling them. They are part of our reaction to fear. In a few minutes, when the adrenalin has broken down in our bloodstream, the body sensations will gradually disappear. We will not be thinking too much about our feelings because we know the reason for them. The fear reaction is there to protect us from danger; actually if we'd recorded our 100-metre dash we'd have discovered it was a personal best. The fear reaction gives us that extra strength needed to escape from danger.

The fear reaction is at the heart of a panic attack. The sensations involved in the fear reaction and panic are exactly the same – fast heartbeat, increased breathing, sweating, trembling, dry mouth, tingling hands and feet, and so on. Not all these sensations may occur in one panic attack and different people notice different feelings. But basically the reaction is the same. The only difference – and this is a big difference – is that we know why we reacted the way we did to the dogs.

Although a panic attack is exactly the same as the fear reaction, there is no obvious trigger or stimulus, such as a snarling dog or an attacker, to set off the strong feelings. No wonder people with panic are completely bewildered. They cannot see a reason for their powerful feelings and start to think of heart attacks, brain tumours, mental breakdown, losing control and so on. The fear reaction is such a strong one that a sufferer feels there must be some reason and it must be really serious. I think most people faced with strong feelings out of the blue would be really worried that something serious was going on. It is quite natural to think like this.

What has actually happened in a panic attack is that the body's normal fear reaction has been switched on by accident.

THE FEAR REACTION BLOW BY BLOW

Coming back to my original point: the body is designed to protect us. Every part of the fear reaction is there for a reason – to help protect us. None of the feelings are at all harmful – quite the opposite; they are there for our safety. It is the same with panic – none of the feelings can harm us. I will now go through the different symptoms of panic anxiety, suggesting the reason for each feeling.

Figure 4 (below) shows the different parts of the body that are involved in the fear reaction.

Figure 4: The fear reaction

MENTALLY alert, focused on danger
HEAD faint, unreal feeling

EARS sensitive to sound
EYES blurred vision, sensitive to light

BREATHING faster

MUSCLES tension

GLANDS sweating, dry mouth, feeling hot and cold

HEART rate faster

STOMACH nausea

HANDS tremor

SKIN tingling, numbness

LEGS shaking

■ INCREASED HEART RATE

"Surges of fear rippled through my body. I knew this time I would not come out of it, I would definitely die this time. Gasping for breath, my heart seemed to thump. I would feel it to see if it had stopped. It seemed to jump inside of me."
S. R.

Panic and anxiety usually involve an increased heart rate. Eighty-five per cent of panic sufferers report pounding of the heart in panic. For some people, awareness of the heartbeat becomes the main problem. The heart beats faster and can give the impression of beating harder. Sometimes it is irregular or a beat is missed. A sufferer might feel the veins throbbing in their neck. Pain or pressure in the chest may be felt. Sometimes people are aware of fast heartbeats as they are dropping off to sleep. Others suddenly awake in the night with palpitations.

Why should increased heart rate be useful to us? The heart is crucial because it pumps blood with its vital supplies of oxygen to every part of the body, right to the outermost parts of the skin. Every part of the body needs oxygen. If we are to fight like a tiger or run like the wind, the extra oxygen in the blood must be sent quickly to the most important parts of the body, such as the arm and leg muscles. To do this the heart must beat much, much faster.

■ UNSETTLED STOMACH

"I get a funny feeling in my stomach and I seem to want to run away... ah... it's a queer feeling, you know."
Edward P.

In danger, who needs to digest their food? The body diverts blood away from the less important parts, the stomach and gut, to feed the more important parts, the muscles of the arms and thighs, so that we can run fast. This can give a nauseous feeling – butterflies in the stomach – or a rumbling stomach. Bowels and bladder get ready to empty, giving feelings of wanting to rush to the toilet (although people do not actually empty their bladders in panic).

■ NUMBNESS AND TINGLING

Blood is reduced from the skin, fingers, and toes so that it can flow into the arms and legs. We may seem to go paler, feel as if the blood is draining away from us or get tingling sensations or numb feelings in the outer parts of our body. Apart from increasing blood flow to the muscles, cutting down blood to the skin is also very useful if we are seriously cut or gashed. Less blood is lost.

■ BREATHING DIFFICULTIES

"Already I was finding it difficult to breathe and the horrible feelings in my stomach started. It was horrible not being able to breathe, I was gasping for air, then I would start noticing the street and houses looking strange."
T. I.

In panic, our breathing speeds up. It needs to do this to get more oxygen into the lungs (which are surrounded by blood vessels), so that more oxygen can get into the bloodstream, and can be taken on to the muscles. This faster breathing results in feeling short of breath or smothering sensations. Fifty-three per cent of panic sufferers report breathing difficulties in panic and 48 per cent smothering sensations. The chest wall tightens, causing feelings of pressure or pain in the chest, or a heavy feeling. Some people think that they cannot get enough air into their lungs and try desperately hard to suck in more air. If the oxygen we breathe in is not used up by fighting or running, then we will have too much oxygen in our blood, causing some unusual sensations such as tingling in the fingers or toes (38 per cent), light-headedness or unreality feelings (45 per cent). Fear of not getting enough air in and taking deeper breaths to make up for it actually gives us too much oxygen.

In what way is this useful to us in fear? If we are to run fast, we must get as much oxygen to our body as possible. Fast and deep breathing does that. You sometimes see athletes deep breathing before a race to increase oxygen to their bodies, to help their performance.

■ SHAKING

"I went into the bingo, and I couldna concentrate. My hands started shaking. I tried to mark the number off the card. I couldna do it, and I telt mysel, 'Dinna be sae stupid.' I couldna see the number, you know, and my hands started shakin' and everything."
Ann P.

Trembling and shaking occur in 70 per cent of panic sufferers. They are simply a result of adrenalin, increased arousal and having the energy and tension to cope with danger but no outlet for it.

If we do not run or fight, then too much oxygen goes to our legs and arms, making them tremble or shake, or giving us wobbly or rubber legs. This is uncomfortable and baffling if we are just sitting still, as we are not using up the energy that nature has provided us with.

Some people with panic have learned a little trick of running fast when they panic – they say it makes them feel better, though it might make other people a bit bewildered! It uses up the extra energy and makes them feel better, but I don't recommend it as a cure for panic. It just locks people into a "we gotta get out of here" routine whenever the first few flickering signs of panic come on.

■ SWEATING

Our glands are part of our fear reaction. We sweat or go hot and cold to stop us overheating and to keep the body's temperature the same – just like a thermostat. Sixty-two per cent of panic sufferers report sweating during panic and 56 per cent report having hot flushes or flashes. The saliva glands in the mouth dry up, making the mouth feel dry. Occasionally people will complain of a strange taste in their mouth, like a metallic or minty taste. Particular body odours may be produced.

■ TENSION, CHOKING SENSATIONS, AND PROBLEMS SWALLOWING

People may feel certain muscles in the body tense up, such as in the arms and legs, feeling a knot in the stomach or tightness across the neck or chest. Tenseness occurs in 68 per cent of panic sufferers. A tenseness in the throat added to rapid breathing, drying of the saliva glands and the coating of the throat sometimes creates choking sensations (61 per cent) or the feeling of not being able to swallow properly.

The increased activity of the muscles can also produce a twitching sensation or trembling. To run or fight, our bodies need to be tense. We do not need to eat when we are escaping for our lives, so we do not need saliva, which is basically in our mouth for the purpose of making it easier to swallow our food.

■ DIZZINESS AND SENSITIVITY TO LIGHT

Often in panic (48 per cent of sufferers) people feel giddy or dizzy, with loss of balance or unsteadiness, feeling that they might fall over. They quite often hold on to something to steady themselves. One man I was treating clung to a bollard on a busy sea front promenade to stop himself (as he thought) falling over.

Sometimes in panic people experience blurred or distorted vision; some complain that it is impossible to read close up.

Have you ever been to an eye specialist and had a few drops of liquid put into your eyes so that your pupils stay wide open and your eyes can be examined more easily? Afterwards, your pupils are still wide open and the world seems a bit strange; you are very sensitive to light; it hurts your eyes; you cannot read and you feel unsteady when you walk. You want to hide in a dark corner until your pupils start to work properly again.

In the fear reaction, the pupils open wide – the reaction comes from adrenalin inside the body, rather than from anyone putting drops into the eyes. This causes more light to flood into our eyes, which is useful to help take in as much of the surroundings as possible in order to spot danger. The muscles at the sides of the eyes that make the eyes focus (ciliary muscles) also tense up, making us focus best on things between three and ten metres away. This is very helpful in battle or if you are attacked by animals but not very useful if you are an office worker trying to read close up. The body seems to have reckoned that, where danger is concerned, it is most important to focus on the middle distance.

■ OVERSENSITIVITY

"I became acutely hypersensitive, unable to stand noise, movement, touch, watching television, the feel of the sheets on my bed, or even the feel of the hair on my head."
J. S.

In anxiety, people can feel much more alert and sensitive to sounds and light than usual. The telephone rings and they are startled and jump up very easily. Feeling so alert can also make people irritable with their families. The story is told of two soldiers back in England from a spell of active duty who were walking down the street; a car backfired and both immediately hit the pavement. It is very useful to be hypersensitive when bullets are flying and danger is around every corner. Adrenalin makes our bodies race faster and our hearing and vision more sensitive. It helps in running and spotting danger but, if we don't use it up, everything can seem to pound away too fast and make the world overwhelming.

■ DREAD

Sometimes people in panic feel a terrible sense of dread or impending doom. As the fear reaction is all about spotting and getting away from death and injury it is not surprising that feelings of doom or destruction come with the package. On top of this is the sufferer's dread of what might happen to them in panic.

■ LOSS OF CONCENTRATION

"I'm trying to listen to the conversation that's going on because you sort of start to drift as you're so intent on yourself. You're drifting into a little world of your own – how you feel and your palpitations and everything."
Y. A.

Being able to concentrate on things such as reading or conversations becomes very difficult, because so much energy is taken up concentrating on bodily feelings.

When panicking, people may also feel that they are not able to control their thoughts and judgments and generally that their thoughts are racing too fast. This is not surprising, as the fear reaction makes us really alert and speeds up the body in many ways, including our thinking. We need to concentrate on where the danger is, and how to escape from it, with all our attention and not bother about logical thought or making well-informed judgments. Again, it seems to be a case of our mind being "preset" into danger mode – blow all the fancy intellectual stuff!

■ UNREALITY FEELINGS

Feelings of unreality or "depersonalization" occur in about 15 to 20 per cent of panic sufferers. They feel that the world is unreal or strange or that they have changed as a person. One man said, "I felt slightly unreal and as though I wasn't part of my surroundings but watching from a distance; my voice sounded strange to me and did not seem part of me." These are very frightening sensations and can sap a person's confidence. Some experts think that unreality feelings are a way of emotionally cutting oneself off from danger, though this is not certain.

IS THE FEAR REACTION SAFE?

There are other feelings I have not mentioned in this chapter that are part of the fear reaction, but I have tried to cover the main feelings. They actually occur and are not imaginary, but they all exist for one purpose: basically to protect us from danger. In panic, many sufferers think that because the feelings are very strong they must also be very dangerous. But what would be the point of having an automatic fear reaction that could do us harm? The fantastic protective system that could help us to react quickly enough to save us from being mauled by a lion could then kill us when we had safely got away! It would make no sense at all. Yes, these feelings are strong – they need to be, to shift us out of danger. But in themselves they are not at all dangerous.

SECONDARY REACTIONS TO HAVING PANIC ATTACKS

Some feelings are not part of the fear reaction, but occur as a secondary result of it. For instance, despair can be caused by the misery of panic attacks. If someone's life is suddenly ruined by these panic attacks, it is normal enough for them to feel that the future is hopeless. Here are four important secondary reactions.

■ INTRUSIVE THOUGHTS

Intrusive thoughts can be very distressing indeed. These thoughts keep coming into the sufferer's mind against their will. They are exactly the opposite of what the person wants to think. They seem to attack the things the person loves most or holds most sacred. For instance, a mother who loves her baby may get thoughts that she might stab or strangle the baby, which of course are most horrible to her. A husband may get thoughts that he might harm his wife. There may be thoughts that the sufferer will do something foolish to ruin their career. These thoughts have an impulsive feeling about them, and people get very afraid if they really believe they will carry out such plans.

Intrusive thoughts can take the following forms:

- Thoughts about actions the person might take in the future, e.g. of harming someone.

- Thoughts about what the person might have done in the past, or something really awful they might have forgotten to do.

- Fears about them as a person: "I'm becoming schizophrenic"; "My memory is going"; "I'm losing control". The person often tries to prove the thoughts are not true by, for instance, constantly doing mental arithmetic or reasoning with themselves until they are reassured they are normal.

- Constant awareness of bodily sensations, or of their own thinking processes, with sometimes quite complex ideas, such as, "If I can't keep control of every thought, I'll lose control and descend into madness."

- Having to count, or to repeat phrases or words continually.

- Nasty thoughts or words running through the person's mind against their will.

The thing that intrudes may come in the form of words, phrases, general ideas, intrusive feelings, or unpleasant images.

Just for the record, these are *thoughts*. Thoughts are entirely different from actions. Just because the thought cannot be controlled, it does not mean that the action cannot be controlled. Actions can always be controlled. Having the thought does not mean doing the deed. Thoughts are independent of actions. It is all absolutely safe.

People who are afraid of these thoughts often try to push them from their minds. The effort involved in doing this means that they are spending a lot of time concentrating on the thoughts, making them more likely to intrude. It is not surprising that during a period of strain and panic more intrusive thoughts are likely, and this can be frightening.

■ FORGETFULNESS
One quite common part of anxiety is forgetfulness. It is not permanent, although the person concerned often thinks it is a sign that they are losing their mind. Partly, forgetfulness occurs because they are preoccupied with their feelings and problems, and other ordinary concerns pale into insignificance. Also, a person who sees forgetfulness as a sign that they are "losing their marbles" may worry more than is necessary. They may notice occasions when they have forgotten things, whereas previously they wouldn't even have thought about it.

■ SUICIDAL THOUGHTS
Depression often accompanies panic. The person may feel low, lose interest in things, lose their appetite for what used to be pleasurable, not want to socialize with others, and their sleep

may be disrupted with early-morning wakening, which is the time they feel at their absolute worst. The future seems hopeless, and one frightening feature of depression is thoughts of escaping the pain by killing oneself. The person may not realize that the awful feelings can change. The ability to tolerate painful feelings, with the realization that, like the seasons, things do change, is an important precautionary attitude. If troubled by depression, it is a good idea to visit your own doctor. They might prescribe antidepressant medication. Some of the medications useful for depression, for example SSRIs, Imipramine, and Clomipramine, can have a beneficial effect on panic attacks.

One variation on this is when the person is afraid that during a panic attack they will lose control and kill themselves or others. This type of thought about harm springs from fear of what they might do, rather than from depression.

■ EXHAUSTION AND FATIGUE

"Putting up with the constant dragging terror saps energy on a massive scale. This results in everyday jobs assuming gigantic proportions, where even to put a load of washing in a machine seems an almost insuperable task."
C. F.

The sufferer becomes tired of fighting and resisting panic feelings, and has little energy left for daily living.

PLEASE TAKE AWAY MY FEAR

In this chapter, I have tried to cover most of the sensations felt by people with panic attacks. They will not all occur in one person but I needed to make the list as long as possible to try to cover most of the feelings that bother people. Panic sufferers at times wish that all these feelings would go away, never to return, or that they could somehow be removed from them, as a surgeon would remove a cancer. However, if we could remove our fear reaction altogether, we would probably be taking away our own life. The problem is that it is being triggered at the wrong time.

I must stress that, in themselves, the body's reactions are natural and completely harmless, though very frightening when the person concerned cannot see what is causing them. An added source of fear is the myths that surround panic, which I shall examine in Part II.

PART II

MYTHS ABOUT PANIC

5

WHAT A PANIC IS NOT!

At its heart, fear is based on the belief that danger is about to occur. One person panicking is afraid of a heart attack occurring, but another is afraid of losing control of the mind and having a nervous breakdown. The idea of danger is always lurking, but different people imagine different types of danger during a panic.

A CASE OF MISTAKEN IDENTITY

Sometimes we make mistakes. Take the man on the underground station in London during the rush hour. A train arrives. It is absolutely jam-packed with people. But he thinks he might just be able to squeeze in – so he does. As he stands with his back to the doors waiting for them to close, much to his amazement someone else pushes in and stands behind him. As he stands there he feels a cold steel point against his back. He has heard about muggings and violence on the underground. Is he about to be murdered? Is he being asked to hand over his wallet? A cold sweat breaks out on his brow. He starts to shake. He slowly struggles to turn and face the fierce mugger, fearing that any moment the knife might pierce through his back... and then... he sees something that quite surprises him. It is a little old lady squashed behind him with the point of her umbrella poking in his back. He has made a mistake.

All the time that man believed there was a mugger with a knife behind him, he sweated, he trembled, his heart raced – he was afraid. On seeing the little old lady, his emotions immediately changed; he was filled with relief, and felt foolish about how he could have made such a silly mistake.

Let me suggest something to you that you may find quite difficult to accept: a panic attack is basically like that little old lady. Terrifying and terrible when you don't know what it is, but absolutely harmless when you know the real cause.

But panic seems such a terrible experience. Something awful must be happening.

Yes, the experience of panic is terrifying. Yes, the feelings are very strong. Yes, it seems to occur for no reason. Yes, sufferers feel they must do something to stop it happening. But it is a case of mistaken identity. The attack cannot lead to a nervous breakdown, a stroke, a heart attack. People do not lose control, pass out or make fools of themselves. It feels as if this is the case, but it simply isn't. In the next few chapters, I want to explore in some detail the myths that people come to believe about panic.

MYTH NO. 1: "IT'S NEVER GOING TO END"

Let's take one of the commonest fears first, that the experience of panic will never end. Panic feelings arise suddenly, and keep getting stronger and stronger until sufferers feel they must do something to escape or stop the feelings. They might run out of shops, if that is where panic is worse, sit down or lie down, do something distracting, call the doctor or take tranquillizers – anything to stop panic mounting. When they start to calm down, they are left with the impression that the attack would have gone on and on, increasing to breaking point, if they had not done whatever it was they did that seemed to stop it. This, though, is an impression. What is the truth?

What is a normal panic attack? Figure 5 (opposite) shows what happens during panic. Panic feelings rise up to an almost unbearable level where the sufferer cannot seem to think straight and just wants to escape (the body's fear reaction). However, if the sufferer does not escape but just faces their fear, panic feelings gradually subside of their own accord.

Based on three psychological studies,[1] in which panic sufferers recorded what was happening to them before and after panic attacks, the average length of attack was twenty-four minutes.

Seventeen per cent of sufferers had attacks of less than five minutes, 40 per cent less than ten minutes, 75 per cent less than thirty minutes and 90 per cent less than one hour.

The body brings panic to a natural end. For the small number of individuals who have panic attacks lasting over thirty minutes, I have often found that their very attempts to fight off the attacks are the main reason that panics go on for so long. They struggle and fight, try to do things to stop the panic, or try to analyse it. These attempts to stop or stifle panic only serve to keep it going longer than it would naturally, and of course this fighting makes the person exhausted. Surrendering to the experience without fighting allows panic to run its natural course. Claire Weekes, who has written some of the best books on anxiety (see the self-help books listed in the "Help for Panic Sufferers" section, page 170), likens this to allowing oneself to be carried along by a wave in the sea rather than trying to swim against it.

Figure 5: A normal panic attack

A panic attack is in many ways like crying. Supposing a workmate or friend has died. You might feel like crying that evening when thinking about it in the quietness of your own home. That is quite normal. If you let yourself cry, you might continue to cry for several minutes or even longer. But even though the feelings are very strong they will eventually calm down. Once you get it out of your system, you automatically stop crying. Let it take its own course and you run out of steam. But what if you fight your grief and try to hold the tears back? You might be successful for a while but then the desire to cry returns. You fight it again – it stops, only to return later. This way you can keep the feelings going for hours. In other words, fight the feelings and they seem to keep coming; but surrender to the feelings, let them run their natural course, and they are over much quicker. It is exactly so with panic. Panic is a time-limited response.

6

DEATH AND PHYSICAL ILLNESS MYTHS

This and the next two chapters try to cover all the main fears about panic attacks. This means that they are crammed full of information. Please feel free just to read the bits that apply most to you.

MYTH NO. 2: "IT'S MY HEART"

"I will have a heart attack. This is the big one. This is the one that will kill me."

Panic attacks in many ways give the impression of a heart attack. Palpitations, chest pain, sweating and breathlessness are common. Panic attacks used to be called "cardiac neuroses" because of their close link with heart symptoms. After a first panic attack, sufferers either check into the Accident & Emergency department of their local hospital or contact their doctors, who comes round on an emergency visit to check the (conscious) person over. Much to the sufferer's bewilderment their doctor cannot find a great deal wrong with them. They do not fit the usual pattern of symptoms for a heart attack. However, "nothing is wrong with you" does not satisfy the sufferer who has just experienced such a terrible attack; and under pressure, or to be on the safe side, the doctor may refer the patient to a specialist cardiologist.

After the usual delays, the person goes through all the tests and the cardiologist reports back to the doctor that there is no heart problem – maybe a slightly raised electrocardiograph

(ECG) reading, but nothing clinically significant. The doctor then tells the sufferer that there was a slightly raised ECG but nothing clinically wrong.

The sufferer may go away with the impression that there is something serious or undetected, that the doctors do not know what they are talking about, or that something is being hidden from them, and they may still harbour the belief that it is a heart condition. And a sufferer given an absolutely clean bill of health is just left bewildered. It had all the feeling of a heart condition – what was it, then?

"It's all in the mind" is unfortunately a phrase that people use about anxiety. Often the sufferer thinks this means that "it's all imaginary". They try very hard to accept that they have imagined this attack, even to the point of doubting their own sanity. But the feelings were absolutely real: "My heart did race, I was breathless. How can this be imaginary?"

Of course, the feelings are not imaginary – temperature change, sweating, increased heart rate can all be measured in the laboratory during panic attacks; these things actually do occur. "It's all in the mind" should really be translated as "the *causes* are psychological", or "the causes are in the mind". The panic reactions are all very physical and very real, but the causes are emotional, not a physical disease.

How can you tell the difference between a heart attack and a panic attack? After all, chest pain, increased heart rate, and breathlessness occur in both conditions. Dr P. Kezdi, Professor of Medicine at Wright State University School of Medicine says:

"Chest pain is one of the most characteristic and valuable symptoms in diagnosing coronary heart disease, but is at the same time the most misunderstood symptom. There are some 101 different causes of chest pain, and coronary heart disease is only one of them. There are early warning signals of heart disease and there are also false signals. As so often in human behaviour, frequently we ignore the true warning signals while being over concerned about the false signals. Let us therefore stress here that there is no way that you alone can determine the true meaning of a symptom or signal. To do so you need the interpretation of an expert, your doctor."[1]

In other words, people should not get carried away by their own diagnosis based on chest pain or palpitations, but on what their doctor or the heart specialist tells them about their heart. Specialists do know what they are talking about! There are, however, certain things that may suggest we are experiencing panic attacks rather than heart attacks.

If they occur in specific situations – such as relaxing in the evening, waiting in queues, thinking about our problems, after a domestic argument – or in particular places – such as shops, buses, queues, churches, lifts, or the hairdresser's – they are very likely to be panic attacks and not heart attacks. Panic is tied to certain cues (even if the person hasn't identified them all); heart attacks are not as closely tied to situations or events.

The one exception to this is exercise. Symptoms of heart disease can be worse the harder we exercise. Panic attacks can also occur during exercise, but they usually occur at other times too. During exercise, such as walking upstairs or walking rather quickly on a cold morning, one's heart is bound to beat faster and harder, and breathing will be faster and deeper. That is only natural, but if this is the only time chest pain* occurs, the person concerned should get a doctor's opinion on whether this might be a genuine heart condition. However, if the person has had a racing heart for some time and is still alive and otherwise physically well, it is more likely to be panic.

Above all, the doctor's opinion as to whether or not someone has heart problems is more reliable than their own opinion. One patient I was seeing was terrified of her heart symptoms. She had pain radiating down her right arm and was convinced it was a heart attack. She had to laugh at herself when I informed her that in heart attacks pain radiates down the left arm!

Another lady I treated typically had panic attacks in bed at night. She thought they were heart attacks, and she would get up, get dressed, and drive eighteen miles through the night, parking outside the city Accident & Emergency department.

---

* Chest pain refers to heaviness or pressure behind the breast bone, or aching or burning between the shoulder blades, sometimes radiating to the neck, jaw, left shoulder, and inside surface of the arm down to the elbow.

She did this so that when her heart attack occurred, specialist help would be available. She had been doing this for ten years! I explained to her the importance of putting this wrong idea to the test. This meant she had to stay in bed and let herself "die" there. It was almost impossible for her to contemplate this horror. But she gradually came round to the suggestion, and after one of our therapy sessions summoned up her courage and decided to go ahead and "die".

It may sound funny but, to her, death was more than likely, so it took great courage for her to agree to my suggestion. After a few excruciating nights of allowing "heart attacks" to occur without trying to ward them off or escape to the safety of the local hospital, she realized that she was still alive and had been fundamentally mistaken about the "heart attacks". After that, the panic attacks got fewer and weaker.

MYTH NO. 3: A MIXTURE OF PHYSICAL ILLNESS AND PANIC

This is a bit more complex and difficult to unpick. It is when there is or has been a genuine physical condition that has now morphed into panic attacks.

When Hilda first came to see me for treatment of her anxiety problems she had already been through a journey of discovery. It had started with an emergency visit to her local hospital with symptoms of palpitations, nausea, and shortness of breath. She felt very unsteady and was terrified of collapsing, fainting, and dying. These are all classic panic symptoms. What marked this out as different from panic was her very high blood pressure (228/112)[2] and the fact that she could not feel her right arm for about two minutes. She had been labelled as having had a transient ischaemic attack (a "mini stroke") and prescribed Candersarton 16mg (for hypertension), Aspirin 300mg (an anti-platelet effect), Simvastation 20mg (to contain cholesterol), and Doxazosin 2mg (to treat her blood pressure). Her own doctor had seen her two days later and referred her to a consultant cardiologist for further assessment. She was given blood tests, an ECG, and an ultrasound of her heart – all of which were normal – but mysteriously she continued to have more attacks, each time necessitating emergency hospital visits. Once, when she was collecting a twenty-four-hour ECG monitor, she collapsed in the lobby of the hospital, was taken to the Accident & Emergency department and kept in overnight. Two further attacks followed in hospital.

"What terrified me most," Hilda explained, "was how long it took the doctors to see me." She had been used to private treatment in Denmark and found the UK National Health Service poor in comparison. "After the first attack in hospital it took thirty minutes for a doctor to come and three hours after the next attack."

I discovered why this lack of care was so important to Hilda. It was because it related to important psychological themes in her early upbringing. She went back and forth between hospital and her own doctor, having more tests, with various changes of medicine.

It was on her eighth attack after another emergency visit to hospital that Hilda made a crucial discovery. "After four hours of waiting time," she said, "a young doctor explained to me and my husband that I was having panic attacks and that I was 'doing them' myself. It was the first time my attacks had been named. I told him that if I was doing them, I would not have another one."

Hilda was obviously a very resolute lady because this was exactly what happened subsequently. She had had the initial symptoms starting on two further occasions but was able to stop them.

"How long have you been free from these attacks?" I asked.

She replied, "It's now just over four months."

It seemed as though I had a patient who had already, in a random sort of way, carried out her own personal experiments and got over the worst fears of panic. She went on to completely recover from panic and never had a further attack.

When I refer to a mixture of physical illness and panic, Hilda's case is still not 100 per cent clear. What was labelled as a transient ischaemic attack had a number of atypical features more common to panic attacks, and the attack had occurred shortly after Hilda had received some bad news about her "adopted" daughter who had betrayed her trust. This fed into Hilda's deep-seated feeling of insecurity, and her panics were increased by the insecurity she felt in hospital in the UK. Hilda's case does show that even if there has been a diagnosis of a physical illness somewhere down the line, then panic attacks are not ruled out.

The National Institute of Clinical Excellence (NICE)[3] guidelines for anxiety show just how entwined panic attacks are with hospital casualty departments. Elsewhere, Huffman and Pollack state:

"The nature of some symptoms of panic attacks, such as palpitations, tachycardia, shortness of breath and chest pain, may lead some individuals to think that they are experiencing a potentially life-threatening event, such as a heart attack. This often results in presentation to A&E departments. It has been estimated that between 18% and 25% of patients who present to emergency or outpatient cardiology settings meet the criteria for panic disorder, which is often not recognized."[4]

MYTH NO. 4: "I WILL DIE"

Over many years my colleagues and I have kept people company when they have had panic attacks. Panic attacks are distressing for the sufferer, and often for the therapist too, but I have never found any serious physical effects from panic, and people certainly do not die from panic. I have searched the research documents, attended conferences, and talked to colleagues, yet have not come across an instance of death from an individual panic attack – and this surely would have been reported.

Some people are afraid that their panic is so strong, so tremendously powerful, that it is bound to cause physical or mental damage – it might set off a heart attack or a stroke. But the body seems to withstand panic attacks perfectly well, time after time, and for long periods of time. The chemicals released into the blood during panic, including adrenalin, are naturally produced by the body, and are basically there to protect it, not to harm it. As Claire Weekes explains in *Peace from Nervous Suffering,* "If you could see how thick and appreciate how powerful your heart muscle is, you would lose all fear of its bursting or being damaged by palpitations."[5] In the same way, though someone may feel pressure or pain inside or around their head, and can feel the veins of their forehead strongly pulsating, the veins cannot burst or cause a leak inside the brain or a brain tumour.

Although it is impossible to die from a panic attack itself, if the person has a pre-existing physical problem such as a history of heart failure or severe asthma, then a panic attack, like other sorts of exertion, might set off their other condition. If a doctor refers people to me for therapy who are suffering from both panic attacks and a diagnosed physical problem, I usually ask the doctor's opinion as to whether they should be encouraged to go through a panic. Most often the view is that the person will experience a lot more panic if left without therapy; overcoming their fear offers them the best chance overall. In cases like these, which are the exception rather than the rule, a gradual approach to the problem may be more appropriate, in which the person only faces fear a little bit at a time.

MYTH NO. 5: "I WILL PASS OUT"

As feelings get stronger, especially light-headedness, dizziness, nausea, and blurred vision, sufferers are sure that they will fall over or pass out – absolutely sure. They steady themselves or sit down to stop this happening. Other people believe them too; shop assistants or helpful partners find a chair for them or help to get them into the fresh air. I have even come across some self-help books on anxiety that misinform readers that "the worst that can happen is that you will pass out". People do not pass out with panic.

Someone may say, "I remember five years ago when I did pass out." But did they really pass out? Or nearly pass out? Were they *actually* unconscious? People may actually have fainted in the past because of some other physical cause – such as passing out in pregnancy because of low blood pressure or anaemia, or a sudden drop in blood pressure, after a sauna or standing up too quickly – not due to the panic attack itself. These physical causes may not be present now, but because sufferers have fainted in the past they may assume they will pass out again. However, it is impossible to pass out from panic attacks.

There is one exception to this rule. It concerns people who are extremely anxious with anything to do with medical matters – hospitals, injections, the sight of blood. Usually in panic attacks the body is getting more worked up and tense as the heart rate speeds up, breathing gets faster, sweating increases and so on, and therefore the blood pressure goes up. However, it is when blood pressure goes down that a person can pass out.

When some individuals see blood, their heart rate and blood pressure go down. It is not only in comedy films that medical students new to the operating theatre pass out at the sight of blood; in real life too people can pass out at the sight of blood or injections. In time, they can learn to overcome this, as some surgeons will tell you. However, this exception to the rule only occurs in a small percentage of people. During panic attacks, a tensed-up person cannot possibly reach such a pitch that they pass out; the body does not work like that. They are too uptight, aroused, and overreacting to be able to faint.

When I wrote the first draft of this chapter discussing passing out due to panic, I said that there were two exceptions to the rule. The second exception was going to be those people who seriously over-breathe during panic. Then I came across an interesting study by three Dutch researchers.[6] They instructed twenty volunteers to forcefully over-breathe for ninety minutes or more. They report: "All our subjects hyperventilated to a degree that is about the maximum that human subjects can accomplish (a reduction in carbon dioxide by 55 per cent) and they did so for one and a half hours. None of them fainted and none of them died." This suggests that it is almost impossible to pass out, even with serious hyperventilation, even though the person may feel light-headed.

MYTH NO. 6: "I AM GOING TO HAVE A STROKE"

A person may mistake a panic attack for a stroke, or think it will reach such terrible heights that they will have a stroke. Others are more afraid about how they will be left after this supposed stroke: they will become "vegetables", unable to cope for themselves, talk or feed themselves, with others having to take them to the toilet. Often they have observed some elderly relative after a stroke, maybe physically deteriorating in a home or hospital, and this has made such an impression on them as to set off a secret fear that this may someday happen to them. Having to depend on others is a terrible thought to them; and needless to say their fear causes them to take a massive leap in their imagination so that they see themselves totally incapacitated by a panic attack. But no such thing actually happens.

MYTH NO. 7: "SOMETHING'S WRONG WITH MY EYES"

"What really got me going were those terrible moments when my vision suddenly went blurred and my heart would leap almost into my throat. Phew, that's awful."

Blurred vision, not being able to focus properly or a general feeling that things are swimming around can lead people to think they have some serious problem with their eyes or are going blind. I have never treated a person made blind by panic. I have never read of a person made blind through panic. I have never met a blind person whose blindness was caused by panic. It would be extremely difficult to understand how the optic nerve, a very tough and thick fibre, could be harmed in the slightest way by a fear reaction. I have seen plenty of people with a fear of blurred vision and what it signifies, but no permanent harm can be done to the eye by panic attacks.

7

THE DESTROYED-BY-YOUR-OWN-BODY MYTHS

Chapter 4 talked about the perfect design of the body. The destroyed-by-your-own-body myths work almost in reverse. Instead of the body being there to protect, preserve and help us, it is seen as an enemy. During a panic attack, the sufferer becomes afraid about some vital aspect of the body's functioning, such as not being able to breathe, swallow or move. Their attention may focus on this area of the body and create a vicious circle in three ways:

- They notice every single blip, quiver, or movement in that part of their body.

- They may try to compensate; for instance, if they feel they cannot get enough air in they may try to suck or gulp in more air. This "compensation" actually increases the discomfort and interferes with the natural (automatic) working of the body.

- Fear of not being able to breathe, swallow, urinate, and so on actually creates more of the feelings of which they are afraid. For instance, fear of not being able to swallow dries up the saliva, making it more difficult to swallow – a self-fulfilling prophecy.

MYTH NO. 8: "I'LL BE PARALYSED"

"I was into Woolworths and then I went up the stairs to get this message (item of shopping). I looked round and there was a crowd of

*people. I picked up the item and was about to move to the counter to
pay for it and I couldn't move. I felt my legs like lead!"*
J. ST.

A feeling of paralysis and a fear that it might continue to some
very dangerous point occurs with some panic sufferers. Again,
these are fears of what might happen but does not occur. They
are based on brief sensations of feeling paralysed, which are
misunderstood and blown out of proportion. For instance, it is
quite a common experience for ordinary people to wake from
sleep with a feeling of paralysis – that they cannot move or
breath. It is very unpleasant, but is only a passing feeling that
disappears as they wake properly. If someone starts to believe
they really could be paralysed forever, they are bound to become
fearful.

One of the standard tricks that stage hypnotists perform on
their audience at the start of a show is to ask them to clasp
their hands together. The hypnotist confidently claims that
they will not be able to release their hands. What happens is
that our knuckles naturally lock and create a bit of resistance
when we try to unclasp our hands – but of course we can pull
harder and release them. Some people, on feeling that first bit of
resistance, say to themselves, "It's true. I can't release my grip.
I am hypnotized," and auto-suggestion takes over from there.
These are the people the hypnotist picks for his guinea pigs –
he knows they will respond best to his suggestions. Thoughts
about paralysis are like this too. If we say, "I am paralysed. This
won't stop," we can overreact and convince ourselves that the
feelings of paralysis will go on forever. But as with most of the
strange feelings associated with panic, they do pass without any
physical harm at all.

MYTH NO. 9: "I WILL CHOKE"

When I described the fear reaction in Chapter 4, I mentioned that
choking sensations and coughing were part of a safety network

to keep us from harm. There are certain physical changes to the throat and mouth occurring during panic attacks that are part of the body's normal "fear reaction". Muscle tension plays a big part in feelings of choking. None of these changes are dangerous. Though they can give the impression that the sufferer might die, muscles cannot possibly constrict to the point of choking a person to death.

Sometimes the sufferer tries to compensate to avoid choking by eating food slowly and swallowing very carefully. Some people eat only "sloppy" food, avoiding meat, nuts, or anything that might get stuck in the throat. Unfortunately these "compensations" change something quite automatic into a controlled and thought-about activity. This tends to destroy the natural rhythm of the body, making the person more likely to choke than if they ignored the problem.

MYTH NO. 10: "I CAN'T SWALLOW"

During a panic attack, the sufferer may focus on the changes to swallowing that are part of the fear reaction – as mentioned earlier, not much saliva is produced in the mouth or throat during fear, which makes the mouth go dry and gives rise to difficulty in swallowing. The sufferer may become frightened that their swallowing will be permanently impaired or that they will not be able to swallow food. Some compensate by doing a test every few minutes – swallowing just to check that it works. Again, this destroys the natural rhythm of the body and makes it more painful and difficult to swallow. This is not dangerous, but makes eating uncomfortable.

MYTH NO. 11: "I CAN'T BREATHE"

In fear and panic, the body is trying to take in more oxygen, so naturally there will be changes to the sufferer's breathing, such as breathing faster. People may start to focus on these changes and become afraid about their breathing. They may feel that they cannot get enough air in, or that they may over-breathe and cause themselves harm, or that their breathing will stop altogether. They may feel they have to keep a careful watch over their breathing or make sure they are breathing in enough air. All this puts a perfectly normal and automatic bodily function under voluntary control, and fear itself increases the breathing rate. Breathing works best when ignored and left to its own devices. The body is amazing at keeping the perfect balance of oxygen/carbon dioxide in the blood.

8

MENTAL MYTHS

MYTH NO. 12: THE DEPTHS OF BLACK MADNESS?

People are often afraid of losing control and going mad during a panic attack. One patient put it like this:

"The fear is that I am going crazy, I am going mad, that this is going to be the worst attack I ever had. And that this attack is going to be so bad that I can never recover from it, and I will have a complete, uh, just lunge into the depths of black madness, you know, from which there is no recall. And I am taking very short, rapid breaths. I am breathing like that and you know the world is closing in on me, and this is the end, you know, there is no way out. I just want to run and get the hell out of there."[1]

As panic gets stronger, and especially if they start to feel disconnected from their body, confused or unreal, people may assume this is the start of madness, and of course they will fight hard to stop themselves entering an overpowering insanity that seems to be sucking them in forever.

Psychiatrists have for many years distinguished major mental illness – the "psychoses" (such as schizophrenia and bi-polar disorder) – from the "neuroses", which are basically anxiety conditions. The term "neurosis" is now rather old-fashioned. It suggests an illness – which panic is certainly not. It is also used in the negative sense of a "neurotic person", which is unhelpful. But whatever phrase we use, anxiety conditions are different from major mental illness. In anxiety, basically the sufferer is absolutely normal, although there is a pocket of experience and emotion that they cannot control in the way they would like to. This is not connected with psychotic mental illness, which involves major changes in thinking and behaviour, such as hallucinations, delusions of grandeur or of being persecuted, or the inability to think logically.

The many people who have allowed a panic attack to run its course without trying to reduce or stop it have found that although they temporarily lose their usual grip on their emotional life, the feelings soon right themselves and they are left unscathed and perfectly sane – like the emotional release of crying mentioned in Chapter 5. *Fear* of mental illness, or fear of losing control of thinking and judgment, rather than mental illness itself, is the problem. A panic attack does not propel someone into mental illness. It is not a sign of mental illness or the start of mental illness. It is an emotional rather than a mental problem.

MYTH NO. 13: "I'M OUT OF CONTROL"

The common factor in this group of myths is that the person will lose control of certain bodily functions, or of their judgment, and do something awful or embarrassing.

"I will do something foolish – start to babble, scream, vomit, wet myself, or in some way socially embarrass myself."

Some people are very conscious of how they may appear and what others may think of them during a panic attack; what stupid and embarrassing things they might do. The sufferer assumes the whole world must notice them because the sensations feel so strong. However, most people in the streets or at work are so busy leading their own lives and doing their own thing that they are not really aware of others.

It is rather like having an ulcer in your mouth. It feels enormous until you look at it in the mirror, and then you see it is the size of a pinhead. The fact that feelings are so strong does not mean that they are strong or important to others, or that it is obvious in the way one looks.

Some sufferers happen to catch sight of themselves during a panic in a mirror or shop window and are thoroughly amazed at how normal they look. They are not that interesting to the average woman or man in the street, scrambling to do the shopping last thing before the shops close, or agitated by the children squabbling. Even if passers-by do notice something, such as a reddening of the person's face, they are more likely to make sense of it by saying to themselves something like, "That person looks hot," or, "I wonder if they have high blood pressure."

Some people think that they will somehow lose control of their bodily functions and wet themselves, or vomit, as their feelings become stronger. Others imagine that their speech will become scrambled and they will speak gibberish. Others have a mental picture of themselves reaching such a pitch that they run around screaming, berserk, out of control, bumping into people and things, thoroughly making a fool of themselves, with people staring at them all the while. Still others picture themselves losing control of their reason and having no more control of their actions, entering a nightmare world in which they have completely lost control of themselves and become as helpless as a baby.

These are tricks of feeling and imagination. They do not actually occur. It is important to distinguish feelings of losing control with actually losing control of one's actions. In the human body, feelings and actions have two different parts of the nervous system devoted to them – the autonomic part (feelings) and the skeletal muscles (actions). The two operate completely differently. People do not have as much control over what they feel, but they do have control of their actions, even though their mind may trick them into thinking they will lose control.

■ VOMITING

"Whenever I got close to a shop, even the thought about going into it, I started to feel hot with a horrible nauseous feeling and I thought, I can't go in. I just couldn't risk being sick in front of all those people."

I have occasionally heard patients say to me that they worried so much about something that they did actually vomit. The feelings of increasing nausea that some people experience during panic easily leads them to think that they might vomit, which would be terribly embarrassing.

Much of what was said about passing out applies here. Has the person really vomited in the past? Was there some accidental cause in the past connected with panic, such as food poisoning? Most people with this fear do not actually vomit when they put themselves to the test and allow themselves to go through a panic. However, a few people do report that they are actually sick through fear. Sometimes they make themselves sick in order to get it over with, through fear that they might be sick! Sometimes the so-called "vomiting" is only regurgitation of food. For those people whose major symptom during a panic attack is nausea, it is unlikely that they will vomit.

■ GOING TO THE TOILET
"When I was going anywhere, I found that as long as I knew where the toilet was, I could manage fine. But I hit real problems when I had to go somewhere new. I'd be thinking all the time, 'What if I can't find a toilet in time?' and in no time at all I'd feel really desperate for the loo."

Wetting oneself is another type of socially embarrassing fear; as panic surges the most noticeable thing for some people is the strong desire to go to the toilet. The obvious fear to occur to them is, "Supposing I wet myself? That would be dreadful." The thought becomes almost a certainty in the person's imagination.

However, despite strong sensations in the bowel and bladder, people do not wet themselves or defecate during panic. Most people have learned terrific control over their bladder and bowels from childhood upwards; if our control was really so poor, how is it that, as adults, we can control our bladder even during the deepest of sleeps? Why should all this change so that we wet ourselves when afraid?

However, some people do have a pre-existing physical problem with their bladder and can have "accidents" when, for instance, moving too fast. In this case panic may be one of many situations that can cause a problem.

■ HARMING OTHERS

"In the evening, I would get home from work and do all the usual things… you know, have tea, watch the telly, but sometimes this panic feeling just crept up on me and straight away I'd be up and out of there. I'd get in the car and drive and drive till I felt it was safe."

This man was afraid that if he had a panic in his house he would do harm to his wife, so he got into his car and drove far away so that it would be impossible to harm her. That was his firm belief. Some panic sufferers are afraid that the feelings will mount to such terrible heights that they will lose control over themselves and kill or injure their loved ones, or other people, or themselves; or not know what they are doing and walk into a bus, or jump out of a moving train. They have misunderstood lack of control; they think that because they cannot control their emotions in the way they would like, they will not be able to control their actions. But the two are quite different. People do not harm those they love during panic. Their emotions may seem to go haywire but sufferers always retain control over their actions. If someone is worried that they might injure others, it suggests they do not really want to do it. Worry or fear is the problem, not that they will really attack or injure their loved ones.

A PAPER TIGER?

In the last four chapters, we have looked at many of the common fears that people have during a panic attack. Any of these fears, or combination of fears, is perfectly reasonable if people have sudden and unbearable feelings that they haven't experienced before. I think anyone could jump to the same conclusions if they experienced the sudden, unexplained, powerful feelings that make up a panic attack. But, even though these explanations involving fear of various disasters, physical and mental, are reasonable and logical enough to explain the feelings, they are simply wrong. Sufferers are not mad or stupid to think these things. It is just that they have misunderstood what panic feelings are. In fact, a panic attack cannot mentally or physically harm the sufferer in any way at all. It really is safe – like a deadly looking snake that is in fact quite harmless. No poison. No bite.

Why is it, though, that one person fears one thing during panic and someone else fears something completely different? The panic feelings are pretty much the same for both people but one may fear that a panic is a heart attack, whereas the other may fear it is mental illness. Why don't they fear the same thing?

One man I saw for treatment of panics could not understand why he should fear that he would stop breathing, pass out, and die during panic. On learning his story, though, it was clear to me that the idea of illness, death, and breathing problems was a strong one in his family. He remembered that when younger, his brother had struggled for air with bronchitis during the night and he had believed that at any time he might die. His father had died of pneumonia. He had recently witnessed a cousin have a very disturbing asthma attack, during which she could not breathe properly and went blue in the face; he himself was rather overweight, and he puffed and panted under exertion. His connection with illness and breathing problems was clear, and it was not hard to see why when he first experienced a panic attack he immediately thought, "I won't get enough air – I'll die."

Another lady I treated feared that during a panic attack the men in white coats would come to take her away to a mental hospital. As a child her family had often told her how similar she looked to Aunt Elizabeth (who had died in a mental hospital). Unsurprisingly she had always harboured a secret fear about mental illness and, when panic attacks started in her life, she automatically labelled them as impending madness.

This sort of experience can often influence a person's ideas about panic attacks. Not every case can be explained by past experiences like this, though. Sometimes a certain feeling that is very strong, such as a fast-beating heart, can naturally suggest to the person a heart problem rather than being related to any pre-existing fear.

For whatever reason, one person can fear one thing about a panic attack and another can fear something completely different. The only thing the two explanations have in common is that they are fears of some disaster happening. We could even say the person has come to believe in a lie, or that their feelings have tricked them into believing that they are in danger. Psychologists often call this "catastrophizing".

Is panic all in the mind? No, not at all. The physical sensations are there all right. But the idea of what might happen during panic *is* in the mind – in the imagination.

PART III

ROOT CAUSES

9

LIFE EVENTS

When panic attacks first occur, they are often out of the blue, spontaneous, with no obvious reason. The person does not do anything unusual on the day they first occurr and does not seem to be under more stress than usual. It appears to be a complete mystery why suddenly panic strikes. Even after panic has unfortunately become part of someone's lifestyle, they may still be puzzled as to why panic attacks occur on some days and not others.

THE INVISIBLE CORD

Although a sufferer may see no obvious reason for the first panic attacks, there is usually a connection with events in that person's life. The person may miss the connection entirely, which is why I call it an invisible cord. However, the connection is there. One of the reasons for this failure to connect events is that the person is looking in the wrong place. Usually when we experience very strong sensations we look around us to see what is causing them at that moment. Is something threatening me? Am I in danger? Have I got a dangerous illness? Or we may connect panic with what has happened in the last hour or two. What did I eat? Was I poisoned? Have I caught a terrible virus? Sufferers rarely look further back than a day to explain their panic attacks. This is why they fail to make the correct connection – they are using the wrong time frame.

Sufferers should not look for a connection in terms of what has been happening that hour, that day or even that week. They should look at the events of the previous one to nine months. It is not the close-up shot that counts; they need to put the zoom lens on and look into the middle distance. Most patients I see, when asked if there was anything important going on in their lives at the time of their first panic attack, will say "no"; but as they describe the months before that first panic, they report all kinds of events – parents dying, a marriage breaking up, a job loss, or an operation. To the outside observer, it is obvious they have been under stress, but because the panic attack did not occur at exactly the same time as the stressful event, the connection escapes them.

WHAT'S YOUR STRESS?

There are many studies showing that in the months before the first unexpected panic attack, the sufferer had been going through a period of stress or trauma, or several things had happened that heaped up on top of each other. Here are some of the common stresses:

- Death or illness of a partner, close relative, or friend.

- Illness, operation, or disability of a partner.

- Marriage problems – arguments, separation, return after a period of separation, a violent or very critical partner, self or partner having an affair, divorce proceedings.

- Children – having a baby, miscarriage, stillbirth or abortion; illness or accident with children; grown-up child leaves home; pressure of looking after a young family.

- Family – having to look after an ageing parent; over-control or meddling from parents in your life.

- Moving away from home, starting a new job or college course, moving to a new house or new area.

- Your own physical health – an operation, illness, disability, or menopause.

- Disasters/accidents – being in a car crash or accident; seeing others hurt (for example, just missed by a speeding car).

- Work – too much stress at work, deadlines, more

responsibility, long hours without breaks, boredom, bad atmosphere at work, failure to get promotion, too many hassles on job, redundancy, threats of redundancy, retirement.

- Business failure, money worries, mortgage problems.

- Taking illegal drugs or legal medicines (as many as 10 per cent of initial panic attacks are set off by taking drugs; see, for example, the personal account of a GP whose first panic was set off by smoking cannabis as a student).[1]

- After-effects of an illness or virus.

Some of the less tangible causes of stress that researchers have drawn attention to are as follows:

- Separation experiences, such as leaving home for the first time, separation by a partner dying, or moving away from home and friends.

- Being trapped, for example in an unhappy marriage or an overly stressful job, or having to live with in-laws.

- Losing control of important parts of your life, for instance your job or your social life.

- Being controlled by a parent or partner.

Almost any of the above stresses may be enough to set the scene for panic. Often one problem on its own is not enough, but two or three problems can pile up to create "system overload".

BUT WHY DID THE PANIC STRIKE JUST THEN?

A common reaction to this idea is, "OK, if there was a period of stress in my life over months, why did the panic strike on 3 June? Why not a day earlier or later? Why not 1 May?"

■ LOWERED RESISTANCE
One researcher[2] carried out a survey of panic sufferers and found that one or more of the long list of stresses described

above occurred in the few months before panic attacks first happened. He also discovered that for 60 per cent of the sufferers he studied, there was a period of lowered resistance just before the first panic attacks occurred. This included the following:

- delayed air flight, causing exhaustion

- menopausal flushing

- an irregular period

- inner-ear inflammation

- flu.

The birth of a child is also a common time when a woman's physical and emotional stamina is low and she is made more vulnerable.

■ RELAXING
Another odd thing, which often throws the person completely off the scent, is that the first panic attacks may occur during a time of relaxation, a long-awaited holiday, or after a bad period of stress is over. It is as if the stress has been building up, then the person relaxes and – bang! – panic strikes.

■ A LITTLE TRIGGER
Apart from the "background" causes of panic there is often a trigger, the last straw that broke the camel's back. For instance, one man who had all his life tried to help his family was cheated and hurt by nearly every family member in turn, eventually being cheated out of the family inheritance. His pent-up hurt and anger about the way he had been treated was the background cause of his panic. The trigger for his first panic attack was a silly little incident – a fuse of a kettle blowing with a bang.

Figure 6 (opposite) shows how panic is set off.

Figure 6: How panic attacks start

TIME PERIOD 6–12 months	1–7 days	instant attack
BACKGROUND STRESS	A little trigger	
Relationship problems, work stress, divorce, death in family and so on	Relaxation/holiday	PANIC ATTACK
	Lowered resistance, physical or mental	

THE RESULTS OF PANIC

I have tried to explain some of the reasons why a panic attack first occurs, but the sufferer may be just as confused about why panic should continue so long (often many years) after the first few attacks. After a few panic attacks, the sufferer begins to predict when or where they might occur again, or what seems to set them off.

Chapter 3 explains how panic begins to change people – fear of more attacks gives them an inner focus in which they are hypersensitive to the first sensations of panic. The fear of these sensations sets up a vicious cycle: fear produces more sensations, which produces more fear, which produces more sensations, which produce more fear, and so on. The reason sufferers fear having another panic attack is the damage they think it might do to them – maybe causing a heart attack, fainting, or madness.

To stop these unpleasant consequences, the sufferer begins to avoid places, situations, feelings, fixed plans, actions, certain thoughts – even dropping off to sleep. So much mental energy goes into avoiding these things that bit by bit their lifestyle changes. And usually they do not like the person they have now become.

TWO CAUSES OF PANIC

Coming back to my original point, there is an invisible world of connections of which panic sufferers are only vaguely aware. They usually do not realize the first panic is caused by stressful events in their life – difficulties or troubles that may have started months before the panic. In the few days before the first panic, there may have been a period of lowered resistance, a trigger event or a period of relaxation that set the scene for the panic to occur.

When the panic occurs, the person does not connect it with the background causes but (not unreasonably) puts it down to other causes: heart attack, nervous breakdown, brain tumour.

Once a sufferer begins to be afraid of the sensations they get in panic, fear of the sensations can keep the panic reaction going, often over years.

This means there are really two main causes of panic:

• The original background cause for the first panic attacks.

• After the first panics, fear of more panic attacks.

But there is another piece to the jigsaw, as we will see in the next chapter.

10

COPING EMOTIONALLY
WITH LIFE EVENTS

"It's so odd. I've never had anything like this before. I was doing so well when all of a sudden my life was taken away from me. I'm all hemmed in by this panic thing."

Katy was mystified by her panic symptoms; they seemed to make no sense to her. They came from nowhere, totally spoiled her life, and wouldn't go away.

Over the last fifty minutes she had described the way her panic had started one year previously. She told me how she would shake, couldn't catch her breath, how everything "blurred over", her mouth went dry, her heart would "take over" her whole body, and how she felt as if she was soiling herself. She was huddled up in an armchair in my therapy office looking small and totally defeated. The afternoon sun streaming through the office window caught her face; it was creased with lines of worry and apprehension. Her eyes looked fearful, like those of a trapped animal.

I thought it would be helpful for her to understand that her panic was not totally random but connected to stressful events in her life. She had already given me a clue to this when she told me that the first panic had occurred shortly after she moved into her new flat with her baby, Ryan. I suggested that it would be useful to explore what was going on in her life at about the time the panic attacks started, to try to make a bit more sense of it.

It was hard for her to focus on anything other than the terrifying symptoms of panic, but after a while she attempted to think about her life in broader ways.

Katy: *"It makes no sense. I was happy and doing all right. I'd never ever heard about panic attacks. Then they started suddenly. How can it be related to my life?"*

Me: *"Well, tell me about the flat – moving to the flat."*

Katy: *"I moved into the flat with Ryan in May last year. I thought it would be fine. I'd got the promise of an evening job as a barmaid, which I thought would get me out and earn a bit of money to buy things, and give me a bit of freedom."*

Me: *"Did it?"*

Katy: *"No. It pretty soon fell through, and then I was stuck all day in the flat with Ryan."*

Me: *"How did that feel?"*

Katy: *"It wasn't good."*

Me: *"How do you mean, 'not good'?"*

Katy: *"It wasn't. It isn't. It keeps... You're making me think now."*

There was a long pause at this point. She suddenly said, "Trapped."

This was like putting building blocks together. At the start of the session Katy had regarded her attacks as a sudden infliction – almost like a fatal illness that had struck her down. Now she had put the first building block in place and noticed that the issue of feeling trapped was somehow wrapped up with panic.

PINPOINTING CAUSES AND EMOTIONAL REACTIONS

In the next session we put together more of these building blocks. She identified a number of other problems that had preceded her first panic attack, and we constructed a list together.

• Having an affair.

• Leaving home (one year previously).

• Having a serious argument with her mother, leading to a severing of their relationship.

• Not being able to pay the rent.

For each of these events I quizzed her on how it made her feel. We made a list together, with important events on the left hand side, and her feeling about the event on the right.

She found it tremendously difficult to pinpoint her feelings about events, but eventually the list looked like this:

Events	Feelings
Moved into flat with Ryan (new baby).	I'm not sure – a lot of different feelings.
Tried evening job as a barmaid but babysitter fell through and I had to give it up.	Depresses me.
Stuck in the flat with Ryan all day.	Worries me. I might have an attack and not be able to get help. Loss of independence.. Feeling trapped.
Had an affair.	Makes me want to cry.
Had a serious argument with Mum.	Makes me angry.
Left home (one year ago).	Also makes me angry.
Couldn't pay rent on the flat.	Don't know. Maybe a bit worried.

At the end of the session I suggested that she show her list to a friend, or someone she could trust, to talk it over and get their angle on things.

In our third session she told me what she had done:

"I showed the list to the health visitor. We went through it together. She asked me why I was angry with my mother. I said she had kicked me out of home when she found out I was pregnant, but started to visit, not because of me but because of Ryan. Then I started to cry for no good reason. She said this must be important for me to cry about it – but I still don't understand why it gets at me so much. Also she asked me if I was upset about Ryan's father not living with me – not really. What will be will be."

I asked her to look at her list again and rearrange it so that the most important event was put at the top of the list, the second most important next, and so on. After she had studied it a bit she put "Had a serious argument with Mum" at the top of her list and said, "I have a gut feeling that this is really important, but I still don't know why."

She listed leaving home as number two. Both of these events made her feel angry. "I don't know how to get rid of my anger," she added.

At the bottom of her list was something that many people would find stressful – "Couldn't pay rent on the flat" – but against the other stresses this was a lesser problem to her.

At this point we had still not identified why the argument with Mum was so devastating, but she was beginning to be aware that a range of powerful emotions was at play, months before the first panic attack happened.

"I want to cry as I'm writing most of the answers. The health visitor says I should cry a lot more. I did a bit when she was here last. I feel I've got everything bottled up inside me and it could explode and I couldn't cope. If I do cry, I feel a bit better, but also it's scary because it feels like a panic attack coming on. I think I should let myself cry a lot more… I usually run out of the room and put on the TV or blast out a CD really loud to drown my feelings."

KATY'S EMOTIONAL PROCESSING STYLE

I have described these sections of the first few sessions with Katy (who later overcame her panic) to illustrate the important role of emotions in the development of panic attacks.

Let's look at Katy. She had a long list of "negative life events": she had a serious argument with her mother one year before, resulting in their separation; she left home; she had an affair; she moved into a flat with a young baby; she lost her independence – she lost social contacts; she could not get out; she was unable to make sufficient money to live properly; and the rent was due.

Katy, like many panic sufferers, had not made any connection in her mind between these events and the panic attack. Why not? Well, there is the obvious point that panic attacks are so physical, so bodily, so somatic, so much like a sudden illness that you tend not to think of emotional issues. Also, there was no obvious connection in time – her panic attack had occurred on 19 May and all these other life events had occurred weeks or months before. So in these two senses, the connection was not obvious. But let's look a bit deeper – at Katy's style of handling emotions, or should we say her style of *not* handling her emotions.

Although she was clearly going through a lot of turmoil she found it very difficult to **identify** her emotions. At first, when I asked her how she felt about being in the flat all day, she replied, "Not good," a very general description of emotional feelings. After quite a lot of quizzing she was able to identify it as "feeling trapped".

When discussing her mother "kicking her out of home" with the health visitor, she started to cry, but said, "I still don't understand why it hurts me so much." She found it difficult to identify and **label** her feelings. She certainly was experiencing great distress – you only needed to look at her face to see the turmoil. She could *feel* all the bodily sensations of that distress – tension, high arousal, breathlessness, heart racing – but did not naturally think in terms of emotional meanings, such as anger, feeling trapped, depression.

As she had not identified and labelled her emotional feelings it made it very difficult for her to **connect** these feelings to events in her life. The last part of the puzzle is that because Katy had not identified important emotions in her life – except of course for fear, which was her constant companion – she had not done anything about the events. She had not tried to work things out with her mother; she hadn't even thought about what had happened, which only started to unravel in her mind as she discussed it with the health visitor.

Consequently she had failed to **express** her emotions, so that when she began to talk to the health visitor and to feel the pain of the issues, the tears started to roll.

Underlying all of this was Katy's attitude to her own emotions. They were something of a mystery to her: "Each time I feel tears starting," she said, "I usually run out of the room and put on the TV or blast out a CD really loud to drown out my feelings."

For her, negative emotions were scary and to be run away from rather than felt and expressed. This had probably been her style of handling emotions from her teenage years upwards. In other words, her style of *not* dealing with emotions was in place long before the first panic attack occurred, and this style ultimately made her vulnerable to having panic attacks.

Once her panic attacks started, all her negative feelings – sadness, feeling trapped, anger – and all the positive ones too took second place to the one dominating emotion: fear. It's as if fear filled her personal world and blanked off everything else.

11

WHY DO PANIC ATTACKS HAPPEN?

Katy was not the only patient who had failed to connect her first panic attacks with important, stressful events in her life. When I first started interviewing panic sufferers I kept noticing the same sense of mystery about the first panic attack – "My life was perfect before then", "It was normal", "I was happy up to that point" – when further questioning revealed it was far from perfect, normal, or happy. I also kept noticing the fear and dislike of emotions that was often expressed. It is easy to understand why people would want to avoid feelings of fear and panic, but this avoidance seemed to cut across the whole spectrum of feelings.

One lady said:

*"I feel butterflies in my tummy and I feel I want to cry. Then I suppress my feelings. I take a great big breath, hold it in, tense myself, or put my mind on something else – take the dog out for a walk, do the housework. I say, 'Don't be so b***** stupid, pull yourself together.'"*

Another man said:

"I allow myself to feel something in myself like sadness, crying. I go so far down. It's bubbling in my eyes, and I try to stop it and shake off what I am thinking. I don't like starting because I get really hysterical. The last time I did, then I ended up punching a wall."

In both cases, these panic sufferers, like Katy, were highly uncomfortable with feelings of sadness, almost regarding them as abnormal or wrong.

Were these chance observations? Was I hearing my patients correctly? I decided to investigate this a bit more thoroughly and, along with my psychology colleagues at Aberdeen, put together a research study aimed at comparing the emotional styles of panic sufferers with those of individuals who had never experienced a panic attack. Fifty patients who had been diagnosed as having "panic disorder", and who came to our department for therapy, were asked to fill in identical questionnaires designed to tap into various aspects of emotion. At the same time, 120 "healthy" volunteers from the Aberdeen University Psychology department's Volunteer Panel were asked to fill in the same questionnaires.

After all the questionnaires were gathered, scores put into a spreadsheet, and the statistical calculations run, I was faced with something I had never seen in psychology research before. The differences in scores between the panic and healthy group were so large that the statistical probability calculation had six noughts – in other words there was a million to one chance of this being a random finding.

The biggest difference was the extent to which panic sufferers tried to control their angry, sad, and anxious feelings. They also showed problems expressing their feelings to others, endorsing statements such as "I hide my unhappiness", "I keep quiet" and "I refuse to say anything about it". They were also much more aware of bodily sensations, but at the same time were less sure about what the feelings were. My colleagues and I presented these findings in a clinical psychology journal, *Behaviour Research and Therapy*, in 2004.[1] In this we put forward a theory as to why panic attacks occur, with emotions being at its heart.

THE DAM THEORY

From the last two chapters, we can see that stress, often undetected by the person and occurring months before the first panic, can build up to a level where a panic attack is triggered. In explaining this to patients during psychological therapy, I compare it to water building up behind a dam. The water rises bit by bit over the months, and the pressure mounts all the time.

At a certain point, the pressure becomes too much, and the dam suddenly gives way. Huge columns of water burst through the fractured dam, causing devastation to the land beyond. Panic is like this: sudden and devastating. Unknown to the sufferer, the pressure has been building up for weeks and months. The panic attack appears to be sudden, but it really is not. What makes me uneasy about the dramatic analogy, however, is that it suggests the sufferer, like the dam, is totally destroyed, which is incorrect. The person *can* recover.

Now the question is, why doesn't the person realize the pressure is mounting? Why don't they realize they are under stress, or notice the warning signs in their body: high levels of arousal, poorer sleep, feeling anxious, poorer concentration? If these signs are read properly, they can offer the possibility of preventing a panic starting in the first place.

The problem with the dam theory is that many people experience stressful events during their lives, such as the death of someone close to them, redundancy, or illness. If, as I have claimed in the previous two chapters, stress can set off panic attacks, why doesn't everybody who experiences stressful events also experience panic attacks?

EMOTIONAL PROCESSING: ABSORBING DISTURBING EMOTIONAL EXPERIENCES

Emotional processing is an important key to unlocking this question. The psychologist Jack Rachman described emotional processing in 1980 as a natural process of absorbing and dealing with hurts and stress in our life. "For the most part," he said, "disturbing emotional experiences are satisfactorily absorbed."[2] But when this does not happen, signs of unprocessed emotion appear unbidden in the form of nightmares, intrusive thoughts, over arousal and anxiousness. In 2007, I wrote the paperback *Emotional Processing: Healing through Feeling*[3] to develop Rachman's work and illustrate how emotional processing acts as a sort of natural healing process, allowing us to handle the many things thrown at us by life.

A positive emotional processing style would involve listening to and valuing our own emotions, allowing ourselves to experience emotion – even negative feelings – focusing on the emotional meaning of feelings and expressing feeling through, for instance, talking to others or shedding tears. Emotional processing can be seen as a sort of natural healing process that can allow us to deal with even the most extreme negative life events. Restrictions in emotional processing style may not matter greatly if there are not too many distressing events in life. However, faced with multiple stressors such as those in Katy's life, the lack of ability to process the distress allows arousal levels to stay high for long periods of time. Unfortunately for her it set the scene for triggering off her first panic attack. In Chapter 4, I described panic as being identical to the fear reaction that had been "switched on by accident". Renowned anxiety researcher David Barlow has called this a "false alarm".[*] There is no external source of danger, such as a masked terrorist, but the fear reaction is the same. *A series of stressful life events, along with an emotional processing style that prevents their resolution, sets the scene for the accidental triggering off of the fear reaction.*

Most modern psychological theories are identical to what follows after a panic attack first happens. If you experience the fear reaction when confronted by a mugger at knifepoint, you know exactly why you are feeling the extreme physical sensations. The sensations don't bother you, but the knifepoint does. Experiencing the same fear reaction when there is no mugger, attacker or knifepoint is an entirely different matter. There is no meaning to such an extreme bodily reaction, so it's no wonder people are terrified, mystified and positive that such bodily symptoms are the result of something extreme, such as a heart attack or mental disintegration. The accidental triggering of the fear reaction almost carries with it the seeds of all manner of fears. All sorts of "fear of fear" loops and avoidance of a myriad of thoughts, sensations and situations described in Chapter 3 then step in and ruin the person's life.

[*] We would like to acknowledge the *Behaviour Research and Therapy Journal* where this diagram was first published. Baker, R., Holloway, J., Thomas, Peter W., Thomas, S. and Owens, M., "Emotional Processing and Panic" in *Behaviour Research and Therapy*, 42, 2004, pp. 1271–1287.

Figure 7: The role of emotional processing in the emergence of the first panic attack*

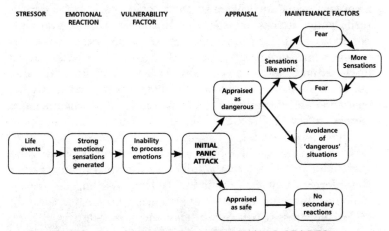

PSYCHOLOGICAL MODEL OF HOW PANIC STARTS

I have tried to illustrate these ideas for how panic initially starts and this is elaborated in Figure 7 above. On the left of Figure 7 are the "stressors", or negative life events, that start the process off. Naturally and quite normally these events generate many strong feelings and raised levels of physiological arousal. This is the second stage in Figure 7 (referred to as "emotional reaction"), which may make sleep harder, all the senses agitated, and make it harder to cope with everyday events.

The third stage is referred to as a "vulnerability factor". Panic researchers have described various different vulnerability factors; in other words, weaknesses that make it more likely for some people to develop panic attacks.[5] Not being able to emotionally process distressing life events properly is one important "vulnerability factor". Katy had great difficulty identifying and understanding her emotional life. I have described this as "inability to process emotions" in the third box. If the strong physical arousal generated by specific events is not dealt with (the "dam theory"), it may ultimately reach a level where the body's fear reaction is triggered off, which is what I refer to as an "initial panic attack" – the fourth stage of Figure 7.

The next box is termed "appraisal" (more of this in the following chapters). Basically this refers to the way in which a person "reads" or "misreads" their panic attack. If the person reads panic attacks as safe, they may persist for a time, but not dramatically change their life. If on the other hand the person "catastrophizes"[6] – that is, they believe any of the myths discussed in Chapters 5 to 8, such as "I will die" or "I will pass out" – all manner of complicated avoidance patterns and "fear of fear" loops develop in their life. I have called these "maintenance factors" in the final column of Figure 7. These vicious cycles of fear have long been known about.

So you can see that the overall picture is rather complicated and there is no one factor that is fully able to explain panic; rather the interaction of many different factors, covering our genes, biological make-up, early life experience, emotional processing styles, life stresses, beliefs, attitudes, and knowledge.[7]

In this figure I have tried to draw together the way in which the main factors interact to produce the miserable condition known as "panic disorder". It is not all doom and gloom, though. By understanding the different elements it becomes possible to do something about each one.

IMPROVING EMOTIONAL PROCESSING ABILITY

In this book I have mainly concentrated on how to deal with panic symptoms once they have become a regular and unwanted feature in a person's life. The promise of this psychological model is that, by improving one's emotional processing style, it might be possible to prevent panic attacks from ever starting, or if they have begun, to minimize the impact of future life stresses on panic.

From this point I would like to briefly turn to what in practical terms might be done to positively develop our emotional processing style. A healthy emotional processing style can help to make us more resistant to future life stresses.

Emotional processing is a bit like our immune system. It needs to be in good working order to protect us from the strains and stresses of life. We keep our immune system in shape with a good diet and proper sleep and relaxation, but how do we ensure our "emotional immune system" is working properly?

■ ATTITUDE

First, it is important to have the right attitude to emotions. This may seem a bit rich coming from an Englishman, renowned as we are for our "stiff upper lip"! During our upbringing we usually pick up unspoken attitudes about emotion: whether it is right to have feelings, how to express them, what is "normal" and "abnormal". These attitudes or "rules" may come from our culture, the community we were brought up in, or our own family, with its individual set of "rules" about emotion. I was first made aware of unspoken rules when I married my wife. In my family, it was normal to tell others what we were doing, even for quite small things like leaving a room. In my wife's family, it was normal for everyone to "do their own thing" and not inform others. Consequently, I would get upset when she left the room without explanation, and she would be annoyed by me supplying unnecessary information about my whereabouts. We solved it fairly easily, understanding that this was the result of two different sets of family "rules".

In some families, the unspoken rules say that emotions should be kept firmly in check; that it is weak or wrong to show emotions. In other families, the rule is that positive emotions are OK but negative ones are not. Some families do not acknowledge or discuss feelings at all. Whatever your background is – and there are many different "rules" – we all have unspoken attitudes about emotions.

So what is a healthy attitude?

• Having feelings and emotions is normal and healthy.

• Having both positive and negative emotions is normal and healthy. At the end of a course of psychological therapy, one patient said to me:

"Before, I wanted everything to be perfect – nearly every day, I was wanting to stay on this happy level all the time. I didn't want to appear out of control to anyone else – angry, unhappy. I'm not going to let this bother me – this 'nothing bothers me' exterior. Now I've come to the regrettable conclusion that ups and downs are normal."

She recovered well, and some months later she sent me a postcard of a jet plane, saying she had finally been able to fly without panicking – her ultimate goal for treatment.

- Experiencing emotions is not usually a matter of conscious control. Rational thinking can be controlled and steered in certain directions, but emotions do not work in the same way and cannot be expected to "obey" us. We do not have to act on them, but it's wise to listen to our feelings.

- Emotions are part of our humanity. If only positive feelings existed, we could not respond appropriately to the ups and downs of life. We would have a fixed grin and be happy whether we won the lottery or our best friend died. The existence of positive feelings requires the possibility of negative feelings too.

- Emotions cannot harm us. They are part of a normal, healthy body.

- Emotions are not primitive or inferior to logic or reason. The renowned psychologist Richard S. Lazarus puts it like this: "We have one mind, and it contains both thoughts and feelings. Passion and reason combine in our mind. There is nothing more human than our reason *and* emotion."[8] What is needed is the right balance between the two.

- Having emotions is not the same as acting on them. *Feeling* anger is not the same as *taking action* – for instance, shouting at, blaming or hitting someone else. There are some situations when action is right and others when it is not. It is not particularly harmful to control our actions, but it can be harmful to excessively control the feeling state.

■ ALLOWING EMOTIONAL EXPERIENCE TO HAPPEN

Generally, it is best not to suppress or control feelings too much, or to switch off or detach oneself from feelings. However, it is understandable that those with persistent, unpleasant panicky feelings would wish to keep their feelings under control. Unfortunately, the habit runs deep, and you can end up trying to control any feeling that stirs, even a positive one. The result is that your whole emotional life gets clogged up. Unfortunately for panic sufferers, any feeling can signify danger. It is as if the whole world is interpreted as dangerous. So for them something more is necessary: they have to learn not to interpret every sensation, every stirring, every feeling and every emotion as threatening. Feelings may not be pleasant, but they are safe enough.

■ PEARLS OF WISDOM

Each emotion contains important information; it is a "pearl of wisdom". This sounds quite wrong, especially for persistent feelings of panic, but in general, our emotions contain information about the world around us, our relationship with others, and our own inner state. Eugene Gendlin, Professor of Psychology at the University of Chicago, has spent much of his career trying to understand how to access the information contained in emotions. He has developed an approach called "emotional focusing", which helps individuals "listen to their emotions".[9] Other psychologists, such as Leslie Greenberg,[10] have produced similar approaches. Here, I will present my version of what needs to be done. This is very simplified; for a fuller explanation it would be worthwhile looking at Gendlin's book on focusing. My version is called "The Three Ls": Looking, Labelling, and Linking.

To make the most of the pearls of wisdom contained in your emotions, here are some simple steps:

Step 1: Looking at your feelings and emotions

The first step is trying to look at your feelings and emotions. You need to be in a relaxed and safe place, free from distractions, to start this. You could ask yourself, "How do I feel right now?" or "How is life going for me?" What bodily sensations or feelings are you aware of? Do not be in a hurry to make any judgments, or to understand the feelings. Just stick with them and focus on them. It is rather like a surveyor conducting a survey on a house, except that you are an emotional surveyor. The surveyor checks the house over, noting its age, dimensions, layout, style, but they are not emotionally involved with the house. They stand back and try to see it objectively. No need to rush. So for Step 1, you just observe your feelings, noting their dimensions, how severe they are, where they are located in the body, how big they are and what their features are. This should be done without getting involved in the emotion, and is what I call "Looking".

Step 2: Labelling your emotions

After spending time observing your feelings, the second step is to begin to put a label on the emotion. Is it anger, or frustration about not being able to speak, or annoyance that your brother always cuts you short when you try to say something important? Each label is tested alongside the feeling to see how well it fits. As you take the label back to the feeling, you are trying to make it more and more accurate. Gendlin points out that simply being able to label feelings correctly can be quite releasing in its own right. This is "Labelling".

Step 3: Linking emotions with causes

The third step naturally follows on from correct labelling. Once a feeling is correctly labelled, it should be possible to link it with the event that caused it. The event may be someone continually criticizing you, undermining you or controlling you, or it could be a realization of how unhappy you are with your job. The emotional feeling provides the clue about the cause. This is "Linking".

For panic sufferers, it may be better to start with emotions other than fear or panic, because it is hard to be objective about something so overwhelming. Perhaps you could begin by concentrating on situations that make you angry or sad. The basic idea is impartial Looking, Labelling, and Linking.

■ **A PROBLEM SHARED IS A PROBLEM HALVED**

Looking at emotions works for some but not for others. Another useful way to aid the processing of emotions is to talk to someone. Talking to a trusted friend, relative or counsellor can help tremendously, and it allows two things to happen. First, it enables you to get your feelings "off your chest", and secondly, it helps you to see things in a different light. The other person might suggest ideas or avenues that you have not considered.

■ **RESOLVING ISSUES**

Once you understand the source of emotional distress, it may be possible to resolve it. For instance, one lady I was seeing for panic-attack therapy realized she had always acted out the role of a subservient child with her father, and her recent bout of panic attacks was related to his attempts to dominate her life again. When she stood up to him, all hell seemed to break loose: he ranted and raved, but she stood her ground. As she learned to assert herself appropriately, she found a more empowering sense of identity, and the panics started to subside. Her father backed down too!

■ **TO SLEEP, PERCHANCE TO DREAM**

Emotional processing is in great part unconscious and natural. It all works pretty well when left to its own devices. For many years, people have known of the healing role of sleep. Edward Young (c. 1700) called it "tired nature's sweet restorer, balmy sleep". Freud suggested that sleep is not a passive activity but active in one way. In dreams, the person is unconsciously attempting to work out and resolve problems from the waking hours, like putting together pieces of a jigsaw that have been jumbled up. Not everyone accepts this idea, and it is difficult to prove, but I think it is likely that dreams are nature's way of processing difficult events in our lives.

■ **WORDS, WORDS, WORDS**

Panic can involve a treadmill of trying to understand or analyse what is happening. In a way, it can cause a person to *think* too much. Some Chinese philosophy suggests that a person's life can get out of balance by thinking too much, by being too cognitive, too analytical. It is important to spend time doing things that involve other parts of the brain, such as music, dance, the visual arts, or spending time in the countryside – preferably things not involving words. Worry and anxious thoughts are often in the form of a mental dialogue, so it is possible to be out in beautiful surroundings but actually surrounded by words. In this case it's important to look at the beauty around you and ignore the mental dialogue.

■ **A CHEERFUL HEART IS GOOD MEDICINE**
It sounds rather obvious, but there is a solid body of research to show that doing pleasurable things, focusing on fun and humour and having good times, all helps in the processing of negative events. Whether it works by distracting us from our plight, or by actively eroding negative thoughts, I don't know. I am not suggesting going around purposely laughing, which is a bit fake, and I am certainly not suggesting *trying* to be happy, or that you keep telling yourself, "I'm happy." It is important to be honest about your emotions. The best way to approach this is to get involved in the activities that make you laugh or give you pleasure, to do happy things and let the emotions take care of themselves. I know this is hard when you are in a pit of despair, but it is a start.

All these suggestions can help us to deal with, understand, and connect with the negative events that might be causing our distress, rather than hiding from, denying, or suppressing them.

PART IV

A PRACTICAL THERAPY PROGRAMME FOR PANIC

12

ATTITUDE!

Chapters 12 to 16 describe a series of practical exercises for panic sufferers. They are part of the therapy, not the entire therapy programme. The information about panic attacks, as contained in Chapters 2 to 8, and the identification of causes for panic, in Chapters 9 to 11, are equally parts of overcoming panic. Chapters 12 to 16 provide the sufferer with a practical way of testing out the truth about panic for themselves. It is up to them whether they want or need this part of the therapy.

Before considering this practical side to therapy it is crucial to develop the right attitude of mind. Success hangs on this. The right attitude involves the following:

• learning how to handle good and bad days

• learning how to handle setbacks

• not expecting the miracle cure.

There will always be setbacks. Setbacks are normal. Therapy does not fail because of setbacks. It only fails if the person reacts in the wrong way to them. Let us look at some different attitudes to these practical exercises.

GOOD DAYS AND BAD DAYS

"Bad days" – when depression and anxiety crowd in on a person – are the single biggest threat to therapy. Good days and bad days are common in anxiety and panic. A person will have a day or a few days where things seem almost normal. Then, for no clear reason, those terrible feelings return again. Occasionally this bad spell may last more than a few days – more like a week.

Sufferers may not understand the reason for a bad day and this may worry them. Sometimes bad days are due to a period of change, stress or tiredness; sometimes to a physical illness like flu; sometimes it is premenstrual tension; and sometimes the person has stopped taking the right approach to fears and has gone back to old habits that make things worse. Sometimes there doesn't seem to be any good reason at all for a bad day.

■ BAD DAYS ARE NORMAL

Actually, when you think about it, good days and bad days are common to all humanity, but bad days do not signify anything too special for most people. They may be uncomfortable but people will not think twice about them. But for the panic sufferer a bad day carries a whole different meaning. Sufferers seem to know almost from the point of waking up that this is a bad day – they feel tense and worked up all day, and are in dread of having a panic attack. There is also regret and annoyance when they seemed to be doing quite well and then one of these wretched bad days appeared; just like the "friend" who has the habit of arriving on your doorstep for a chat just at the wrong time. It is important for the sufferer to learn to accept that good days and bad days are normal; not to get too excited about good days, nor too down about bad ones.

■ BACK TO SQUARE ONE

Let us suppose a sufferer has started the therapy programme and has made tremendous strides in overcoming panic; they have just had a week without any panic feelings at all when suddenly a full-blown panic attack occurs. The most usual thought that goes through the sufferer's mind is, "Oh no. I'm back to square one again. This programme is not working. What's the point in carrying on?" But on bad days like this they should not be thinking in terms of "back to square one"; but something like, "I've made progress before, I can do it again."

▪ YOU CANNOT LEARN ANYTHING NEW WITHOUT THE ODD FAILURE

It is rather like learning to ride a bike for the first time. It comes gradually. If, the first time learners fall off, they say, "It's not working – I'll never learn this," they may give up and never learn at all. They must realize that setbacks are part of the learning process, dust themselves off, and get back onto the bike again.

Before this part of therapy starts, sufferers should settle it in their minds that setbacks are normal and should be expected, and work out how they will handle them *when* rather than *if* they occur.

▪ THE COURSE OF THERAPY NEVER RUNS SMOOTH

Progress in therapy will not be even. Figure 8 (below) shows what normally happens when a panic sufferer begins to improve – for instance, if someone were following the self-help instructions in this book or seeing a clinical psychologist for help.

Figure 8: Recovery during therapy

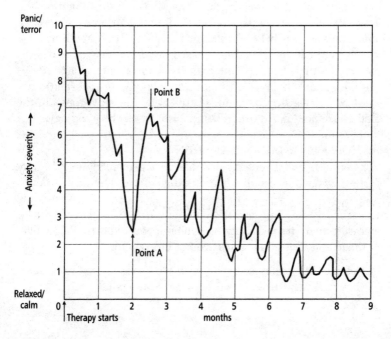

The downward line shows improvement over a six- to nine-month period. But as we can see the improvement is not at all even – there are many ups and downs from day to day – though at the end of therapy panic has disappeared. Look at point A on the graph – let us say that is a Monday – very little anxiety all day. Tuesday (point B) is a bad day: "What's happening? Oh no, back to square one." The sufferer feels demoralization and despair, and feels like giving up. But it is not back to square one; it is only part of the random ups and downs of the body. Overall, the person is improving, but they cannot see this from one day to another. Panic sufferers should take a long-term view of therapy. They must not be swayed by a bad day or a bad week.

■ THE GOOD SHOWS UP THE BAD

As a person gets better they notice bad days more. Let's say at the beginning of therapy someone has panics every second day. Then they begin to improve and have five full days free of panic. They start to feel that life is worth living again and begin to have hope that they really can shake it this time. Then on the sixth day, they have a panic attack. All the old gloom comes back and they can hardly be blamed for thinking, "It's all an illusion. I can never change." But this is based on an underlying mistaken belief. We might call it "the overnight miracle cure attitude" – the idea that our problem must immediately disappear 100 per cent and never appear again. Actually, as therapy goes on, the bad days stand out more in comparison with the good days.

■ TO BE A LONG-DISTANCE RUNNER

The point is that a person must take a long-term view of therapy. They *can* change. So on a bad day the sufferer should:

- Realize it is only a temporary setback.

- Not give up hope. Remember the improvement they have made and that good times are possible again.

- Realize that if they carry on with what was successful before, they will win through and be successful again.

110

THE THREE BUTS

There are three quite common reasons why people will not try therapy:

■ BUT I'VE HAD IT FOR TOO LONG

If someone has suffered for many years, it is understandable that they should feel this. But it doesn't matter if the problem has been with someone two months or twenty years; it is still possible to change. One major book on agoraphobia[1] reviews what factors are able to predict which sufferers improve in therapy and which do not. The authors conclude that "the therapist need not be daunted by patients who are very anxious, are slightly depressed or have phobias of considerable severity of great duration… surprisingly results can be achieved with even the most handicapped or disadvantaged patients". I know of at least one lady who suffered from panic and agoraphobia for twenty-five years but has overcome it.

If anxiety has been with a person for many years, I can understand that hope long ago went out of the window. Sufferers feel better for a day and at first say to themselves, "It's gone!" – but then it comes back again, time and time again, until they despair of ever finding a cure. For some, anxiety is so familiar that when they start to recover they feel really strange, as if they are missing some familiar companion, and almost look around for something to worry about. No one can give a 100 per cent promise of full recovery, but with correct information and understanding and by using the right approach there is a good chance of overcoming panic anxiety.

■ BUT THE FEELINGS ARE SO CRIPPLING

One of the hallmarks of panic attacks is that the sensations people experience are very powerful and seem to increase dramatically once they start. This can become so bad as to make it difficult for them to concentrate or to carry out some of the simplest things in their life. However, when it comes to therapy for panic attacks it does not seem to make much difference how strong the sensations are, how many sensations the person experiences, or how frequently they have panic attacks. The same principles and good results seem to apply across the board. Recovery is not just limited to those with weak, infrequent, or limited panic attacks.

■ BUT I'VE TRIED THIS BEFORE

Sometimes clients say this when this part of the therapy is explained. Yes, they have tried it before but they have tried a bit of this, a bit of that. A bit from this book, a bit from that book. A magazine article recommended this, a friend suggested that. They once tried a relaxation CD, took pills for a while. It is rather like being tossed about by the waves – first in this direction, then in that.

The following are needed:

- Determination – the person must keep going on, day after day, week after week. There will be setbacks, there will be failure. There should be no regrets, no despair, just a "plodding on" attitude.

- The right approach – of course, it is no use someone going on and on in the wrong direction; they end up miles from where they intended. The person must be sure that the direction and the programme is right for them – and then stick to it.

13

THE ANATOMY
OF FEAR

Whether panic attacks were initially caused by being trapped in an unhappy marriage, the death of a child, leaving home, or whatever reason, once the first panic attacks occur, fear usually steps in too.

WHEN FEAR STEPS IN

Sufferers become afraid of having more panic attacks, and afraid of what the attacks may mean. They are bewildered by what is happening to them. In this chapter, I want to go on to examine the fear reaction in a bit more detail to help sufferers understand their fears about panic attacks better and find a way out of this vicious circle of fear. In fact, a sufferer may not have labelled their reaction to panics as "fear". They may call it "discomfort" or "anxiety", or may have been so successful in preventing panic attacks from occurring that they cannot identify a fear at all.

FREEZING THE FEAR REACTION

The fear reaction occurs in an instant, so it is a bit difficult to see what is happening. DVD players have a button on the remote control that allows us to slow down the film. We can slow it down so much that it is possible to look at it frame by frame and observe details that would be impossible, to see when viewing it in real time.

Let us suppose we could slow down the fear reaction like this. What would we find?

■ FREEZE FRAME 1

We would see that the very first part of the fear reaction does not involve the emotion of fear at all. The first part involves recognition.

The psychologist's jargon for this part of the reaction would be that the person first has to make an "appraisal" of danger. In other words, before someone feels fear they must recognize that there is danger ahead. This is what "appraising" danger means.[1]

These appraisals can be very simple sense recognitions involving little thought, such as seeing a snake or flames leaping around us.

These simple types of danger seem to cause a reaction quite naturally in both animals and people. Another common "automatic fear" provoker is loud noise. Great generals throughout the centuries have known this and instructed their troops to shout and scream when they attack the enemy.

Let's take a different illustration. Suppose we are walking down a dark alley in the inner city late at night and at the end of the passage suddenly we see the silhouettes of two men. When they see us they stand perfectly still, waiting at the end of the passage.

Our appraisal involves quite a high level of mental activity. It is based on the knowledge that late at night in cities, where there is little help available and under the cloak of darkness, crimes are committed. And that a person standing still at the end of a path means "blocking my way". And that two male figures who block your way in this place equals danger. Although this appraisal may happen in an instant, it involves thoughts, knowledge, and previous learning.

In other words, before our bodies register fear we must first recognize it. The recognition varies from simple recognition of naturally dangerous objects to thoughts and knowledge about what is dangerous.

■ FREEZE FRAME 2

The next part of the freeze frame concerns feelings or emotions of fear – all those feelings and sensations I talked about in

Chapter 4: sweating, heart racing, breathlessness, tension, trembling, choking sensations, hot flushes, chest pain, nausea, dizziness, numbness, and so on. As I explained in that chapter, these are a fairly standard set of very strong sensations designed to help us to react quickly to avoid danger. The reactions occur quite automatically when we are faced with danger and are common to everyone. Once danger is recognized or appraised (Freeze frame 1) the fear emotions are automatically "switched on" (Freeze frame 2).

■ FREEZE FRAME 3

The third part of the reaction is the way in which we respond. The strong sensations of fear produce a response in us. The most common natural response is to run, to fight, or to freeze. We can, however, learn to change our response to fear. I recently heard a story on the radio in which a twelve-year-old boy was interviewed. He had been attacked by a grizzly bear in the Rockies. He described the bear hitting and clawing him; then he went limp and pretended to be dead. He had heard some trappers a few days before saying that bears stop attacking someone once they think they are dead. He lay still, and the bear did go away. This is a case in which the boy felt all the fear emotions (Freeze frame 2), which naturally made him want to run away, but because of his "inside knowledge" about bears, he overrode the feelings and lay completely still. He was controlling his reaction to fear emotions.

Figure 9 (below) shows the three main parts of the fear reaction.

Figure 9: The three main parts of the fear reaction

1 →	2 →	3
Appraisal	**Fear emotions**	**Response**
Person registers danger	Person instantly feels strong bodily sensations	Person takes action such as running away, fighting

Drawing the reaction like this is rather artificial; we have slowed the frames down considerably in order to take a look at the different parts of fear. In real life, the whole fear reaction is so quick that it seems as if all the different parts of the reaction are rolled into one.

IT'S THE THOUGHT THAT COUNTS

Now here is an interesting and important part of this. Having fear emotions depends on whether we believe danger to exist. If we do not think danger exists, our body will not react with fear at all. On the other hand, if we think danger exists, even though it doesn't, our bodies will react exactly the same way as if danger was really there. It all depends on our appraisal of danger.

Here are some examples of different sorts of appraisal:

- Appraisal of danger when it is *actually* there (see Figure 10, below).

- *Failure* to appraise danger when it is *actually* there (see Figure 11, opposite).

- Appraisal of danger when it is *not actually there* (see Figure 12, opposite).

Figure 10: Appraisal of danger when it is *actually* there

Appraisal	Fear emotions	Reaction	Result
'There are two men waiting for me at the end of this dark passageway. This is midnight in the Bronx.'			
DANGER →	Fear emotions experienced →	Run fast in the opposite direction →	You live to face another day

116

Figure 11: *Failure* to appraise danger when it is *actually* there

Appraisal	Fear emotions	Reaction	Result

'These two men waiting for me must be my two pals who said they'd be there.'

NO DANGER → No fear emotions experienced → Carry on walking towards the men → Death through stabbing

Figure 12: Appraisal of danger when it is not *actually* there

Appraisal	Fear emotions	Reaction	Result

'There are two men waiting for me at the end of this passage.'

DANGER → Fear emotions experienced → Run fast in the opposite direction → You live to face another day, but don't discover the two 'men' were a couple of stray cats sitting on top of some dustbins

Now let us look at a list of things that most people typically appraise as dangerous (Table 1, below) and compare it with the list typical of panic sufferers (Table 2, opposite). What is the difference between the two lists?

What is dangerous to most people lies outside themselves – something "out there" that may harm and kill them. For the panic sufferer, what is dangerous to them is inside them – feelings and sensations. When bodily sensations signal danger, a person looks out for them all the time (the inner focus) – scanning the body for signs of danger. And, of course, many times throughout the day such bodily changes will be experienced. This means that the panic sufferer may be appraising danger several times every day and experiencing fear emotions each time. This is like living in a kind of perpetual hell of fear.

MISTAKEN DANGER

Table 1

Things that many people appraise as dangerous	Result feared
Threatening gang with knives	Knife wounds
Lions, tigers, bears, sharks on the loose	Mutilation or death
Your car goes into a skid	Injury, death
Snakes, scorpions, deadly spiders close by	Poisonous bites
Trapped in a fire	Burns
Experiencing a storm, hurricane, earthquake	Injury
Caught in a current when swimming	Drowning
Crowd on the rampage	Trampling to death
Sudden, severe pain	Serious illness

Table 2

Things (as well as those in Table 1) that panic sufferers appraise as dangerous	Result feared
Palpitations	Impending heart attack
Dizziness	Losing consciousness
Being short of breath	Not being able to get enough air
Feelings of unreality	Losing control of the mind
Numbness	Passing out
Strong feelings in bladder	Incontinence
Feelings of paralysis	Impending death

The panic sufferer definitely falls into the third category of appraisal. They are appraising danger when there is really no danger present. In other words, they will have the same reaction as anyone else when confronted by a thug with a knife. There is nothing wrong with the panic sufferer's emotional reaction – it is all in perfect working order. The only thing wrong is that they also mistakenly think danger will occur when none is present.

Please pause for a moment to see what this means. It is saying that panic sufferers are normal individuals. There is nothing wrong with their mental apparatus. They are emotionally responding to danger as they ought to be. There is no question of mental illness, instability, or insanity. They are normal people who are quite simply making a mistake. They believe that if a panic attack were to be left unchecked, some personal danger would happen to them. Anyone who believed what they believe would respond with the same fear reaction.

The problem lies with their mistaken appraisal or belief. The solution lies with the discovery that panic attacks are quite safe.

PINPOINTING THERAPY

What part of the fear reaction should therapy attempt to change? If we tried to change the fear emotions (Freeze frame 2), this might be harmful to the person; the next time danger arose the person might not react strongly enough to evade it. It

119

would be possible to change their reaction to the fear emotions (Freeze frame 3), as the boy did with the grizzly bear. But even if sufferers changed their reaction they would still experience unpleasant fear emotions. The Cognitive Invalidation approach aims at changing the mistaken appraisal about the danger of panic attacks (Freeze frame 1). When the person knows that panic is safe, they will no longer experience fear emotions as they did before.

14

TAKING THE STING
OUT OF FEAR

How can a person discover that panic attacks, though unpleasant, are safe? Would it be by asking others who have had panic attacks? Would it be by talking it over with a friend? Would it be by listening to a therapist, or an expert on the television or radio? Sometimes sufferers may hear from others that panic is safe and pay lip service to this, but deep down they are unconvinced.

GETTING AT THE DEEP-DOWN BELIEF

What needs to change is that deep-down belief or appraisal. Deep down, the panic sufferer fears that if a panic attack were to happen and was left to continue unchecked something terrible might happen.

They may not be able to put their finger on what that something might be, but it is pretty bad. It may include dying, going insane, losing control of mind and body. Deep down it is a real possibility and it is nasty.

How can one get at these deep-seated appraisals? You cannot easily argue with yourself and force yourself to believe otherwise. Belief is not easily persuaded by such reasoning exercises. The best way to discover the truth of what really happens is by personal experience; sufferers need to discover the facts for themselves. They need to set up a personal "experiment" to test out for themselves whether their belief is true.[1]

THE PERSONAL EXPERIMENT

If scientists set up an experiment, they will design it in such a way as to test out their theory; the results of the study will either disprove or confirm their theory. If they said, "I know the answer already so there's no need to test it out," others would say, "Prove it." If they arranged an experiment that could only show their theory was right, this would not be a proper test – it would be rather like tossing a two-headed coin, which must come down heads. The experiment must be capable of disproving or proving the theory being tested.

What about the personal experiment? This too is set up to confirm or disprove something meaningful from the everyday life of an individual person. Panic sufferers can set up an experiment to test out what happens to them when a panic attack is left unchecked.

ENTERING THE UNKNOWN

A sufferer may say at this point, "But I've been through panic a thousand times. I know what will happen." However, the sufferer is more like a scientist who has never properly tested the theory. Here are some of the things that may hold back that crucial experiment:

- They remember back to the first few terrible panic attacks they had, which seem to be seared into their memory, and are so fixed on these attacks that it is difficult to shift to the present, and what would happen today.

- The fear of what *might* happen is so strong that they assume it *will* happen. This, though, is an assumption, not a proven fact.

- Because the feelings of panic are so unpleasant, they have concentrated on the feelings and not stopped to consider what actually happens.

- They have avoided places, situations, actions, feelings for a long time or used "safety routines" to stop panic starting. So they have effectively blocked themselves off from the crucial question: what would happen without all these precautions?

- Their "lifesavers", which stop panic rising (alcohol,

tranquillizers, phoning for help, sitting down in a quiet place, deep breathing, relaxation exercises, and so on), never allow panic to reach a natural peak, and so they never discover what would have happened otherwise.

This is how one sufferer explained how carefully every aspect of her life was planned so she could avoid anything that might set off a panic:

"I only know that I have been planning like this for many years, to such an extent that it has become part of my life. I am an expert at it. I am superb at thinking on my feet, at tremendous speed, and at telling white lies and making plausible excuses. I am sure that no one involved in my planning has the least idea that they are being constantly manipulated. I don't like the effort involved. The brain power it takes could be so much better used. The thing is that if I just let happen what will, then I am entering the unknown."
Mrs F. A.

In order to carry out a proper test of what happens, the sufferer needs to enter this "unknown", and that requires tremendous resolve, courage, and a bit of planning.

■ **TERRY'S EXPERIMENT**
To get the feel of what a personal experiment is like, let's take the example of Terry, a successful Dundee farmer who avoided going into shops and would not visit anything more than a small town through fear of panic. Terry was fed up with the restrictions his panic imposed upon his life and was sure that it cost him a great deal financially. His case is an example where a single simple personal experiment was the key to his recovery. Many cases are not as straightforward and require a series of personal experiments, each one aimed at testing out a different aspect of the person's fear.

I first saw Terry after he had been referred by his GP for psychological therapy. In our first session, he explained his fears and how they had developed over five years. His life had been getting more and more restricted as a result of his fear. His greatest fear was the large department store in Aberdeen city centre. In the second session, I explained the nature of panic to him and how it was essential to find out what really happened. Rather than gradually approach his problem he wanted to "go for gold" and carry out his personal experiment on the worst fear.

We both went into Aberdeen city centre. I parked my car, and after further "briefing" we both walked into the department store. At first, he walked quite quickly round the store looking intently at everything. I asked why he seemed to be reading every label. "To keep my mind off the panic," he replied – this was his safety routine. I asked him not to distract his mind like this. He stopped reading labels, but still walked round quickly. "Why are you moving around so fast?" I asked. "It helps me not to feel dizzy feelings," said Terry. I asked him if he would stand still. He agreed to stand in one spot. He stood, legs straddled, bracing himself. "Why are you standing like that?" I again enquired. "To stop myself falling over" – his ultimate fear. "I'd like you to stand with your heels together," I said.

This was the crunch point. I had asked him to do just about the hardest task possible. It was the crux of his experiment; the only way he could really test out whether he would fall down through panic. He reluctantly put his heels together. Immediately he did this a wave of panic came over him. But to his surprise he did not fall over as expected, and the panic actually only lasted a few seconds.

After this "crunch" experience, he started to go into many places and overcame most of his fear. He had been afraid to put the ultimate fear of falling over to the test and over the years had done everything possible to avoid this. Once he truly faced the thing he feared most, he discovered there was nothing really to be afraid of.

SETTING UP A PERSONAL EXPERIMENT

Here are the steps a panic sufferer might follow to test out what really happens in a panic.

At the start, the person needs to ask: "What is the thing (or things) that I am afraid might happen if I had a panic attack and didn't try to control it or stop it or escape from it in any sort of way?"

Some people find this difficult to answer. They may say that they are not afraid of anything happening. When I ask clients, "What would happen if you didn't run out of the store when you had a panic attack?" they sometimes reply, "But I would never let it get to that stage." In other words, they have set up such an elaborate system of safety routines that they don't even have to think about what might happen. Sufferers should take away all their imaginary safety routines and ask what is the worst they think could happen. Some of the most common beliefs about panic are covered in Chapters 5 to 8.

Having identified what they are afraid might happen they need to set up a series of personal experiments to discover whether this really does happen. The experiment would involve:

■ 1. PUTTING THEMSELVES IN THE SITUATION THAT MIGHT SET OFF PANIC – NOT AVOIDING IT

This may mean facing the following:

- places

- situations

- feelings

- the anticipation of events

- actions

- thoughts about panic

- sleep.

■ 2. NOT CARRYING OUT ANY SAFTEY ROUTINES LIKELY TO STOP A PANIC HAPPENING

■ 3. WHEN A PANIC STARTS, NOT DOING ANYTHING TO STOP IT REACHING ITS PEAK

In other words, the person needs to allow a full-blown panic attack to occur.

It is only after Steps 1, 2, and 3 have been taken that the person can truly discover what happens in a panic attack. When they discover by personal experience that they don't die, pass out, lose control and so forth, their fears and panicky feelings begin to be eroded. This type of experiment is, naturally, extremely threatening for a panic sufferer. It is asking them to risk their sanity or their life.

I mentioned that Terry's case was a simple single personal experiment. Before we go into any more detail let's get the feel of a more complex situation, in which Ralph needed to carry out a series of personal experiments in order to realize that panic was safe.

15

RALPH: AN EXAMPLE OF SUCCESSFUL THERAPY

The account of Ralph, a twenty-eight-year-old postgraduate student, is a true illustration of someone going through this therapy programme. He is an example of someone with very severe panic who completely recovered. Obviously everyone who experiences panic attacks is unique so no two people's cases will be exactly the same. Ralph's case has much in common with other panic sufferers but differs in certain features. One of the unusual aspects of his case is the age at which he first experienced panic attacks (thirteen years old). This is younger than is typically the case.

I first heard about Ralph when a psychiatrist at the hospital where I worked asked me to see him as an urgent referral. He had been admitted voluntarily as an inpatient to one of the psychiatric wards, at the urgent request of his doctor. The psychiatrist had described him as intensely anxious, with a high pulse rate and profuse sweating. His stomach was churning and he had a fear of losing control of his bladder and bowels and of fainting. The psychiatrist had started him on the antidepressant drug Fluoxetine, and decided to discharge him with the idea of referring him to the Clinical Psychology department for outpatient therapy (the most usual route for panic sufferers). However, Ralph returned to the ward the following day, having had a completely sleepless night with intense feelings of terror. He was given the tranquillizer Diazepam in addition to the Fluoxetine, and the psychiatrist asked me to see him urgently.

SESSION 1: FEAR OF MADNESS

I first met Ralph on the following day. This was to be the first of our thirteen sessions, which altogether stretched over seven months. I asked him to describe what he had been experiencing recently. He felt that any problem in life could push him over the edge. Going "over the edge" meant that he thought he might completely disintegrate, no longer being responsible for his actions, turning into a different person, unable to return to normality. He also described a fear of breaking down in front of others – that he would start crying with no control over his emotions. In the last year, his panic attacks had worsened. "Now I would call them 'terror attacks'," he told me.

He was completely bewildered about why he should be experiencing such terror – there was no particular cause that he could see. In fact he felt he had had quite a happy life in general. The fact that he saw no cause proved to him that he had an "innate deficiency in my personality, which can't be cured". Going into a psychiatric hospital had simply confirmed his own worst fears about his insanity. He said that while he was in hospital he experienced almost constant panic, feeling nothing could be done and that he could not cope. "As if I would explode... I was rooted to the spot with fear."

The point to realize here is that this man was experiencing severe tension, anxiety, and fear. His problem was not insanity, but a fear of insanity, and that fear stoked up more and more anxiety.

■ HOW IT ALL STARTED

I asked him to describe the problem right from the start. The idea at this point in therapy was to get him to put his thoughts in order and discover that there was a pattern and causes for his panic rather than it just being irrational. The sort of questions I asked were aimed at helping him to spot these causes and connections himself, just as described in Chapters 9 and 10.

He remembered his earliest years as happy until the age of five, when his mother was admitted to hospital with a nervous breakdown. She was gone for a long time and he was given no explanation for it. His family moved around the world a lot. At the age of thirteen, when his family was living in Trinidad, he was sent to boarding school in the UK.

He arrived three days before term started. The whole school was empty and he slept in a large dormitory by himself. He was left alone the next day. There were no friends or relatives nearby. Over the next few days other pupils arrived with their parents, but from the start he felt he didn't fit in. The first panic attack was still vivid in his mind. He was sitting in the school hall with many boys around him. Suddenly he experienced terrific fear and wanted to get out. He was confused because he could see no reason why he should suddenly and for no apparent reason be struck with such strong, overpowering emotion.

After this, he began to be afraid of speaking in front of a group of boys, which he refused to do, and he was apprehensive of any new places. Eighteen months later he was moved to another boarding school nearer to relatives, where he felt less isolated, and the problem largely subsided.

At eighteen years old, he went to the University of Birmingham to study economics. He lived with a friend in a nearby flat, and this was quite a good period in his life, when he was reasonably clear of panic. After graduating at the age of twenty-one, he set up his own business, later moving to Cardiff to live closer to his father, who by then had separated from his mother.

When he was twenty-five, the relationship with the woman he had lived with for six years broke up. At this point, he completely uprooted himself, leaving all his friends and the familiar surroundings of Cardiff, and went to live with his mother in Huntly near Aberdeen. He later enrolled on a postgraduate course at the University of Aberdeen and bought his own cottage in a village outside the city.

It was while he was sitting in a crowded lecture theatre in his first week at Aberdeen University that panic unexpectedly returned. After this first panic attack, he became constantly anxious and fearful of more panic attacks, and over a period of time he found that even the most simple tasks became difficult through fear. He dropped out of university and his life became more restricted until it reached the crisis point when he was admitted to hospital.

■ WORKING OUT THE LINKS

At this point in the session, we tried to work out if there was any link between the two main panic attacks he had described at the ages of thirteen and twenty-five. At first, any link escaped Ralph, but by listing the similarities between the two situations he began to see that on both occasions he had been living by himself, isolated from his usual friends and family. In fact, throughout his life he had very rarely lived anywhere by himself but had always had others near him. This was something of a revelation to him. Whereas before he had thought these "terror attacks" were merely random outbursts of his hereditary "madness", now he began to see that there might be some meaning or cause to them. At the end of our (long) first session, I gave him some earlier drafts of Chapters 4 to 8 of this book to take away and read, and we arranged the next session for the following week. He decided at the end of the session that he would go back to live with his mother instead of living by himself in his cottage.

SESSION 2: RALPH'S FEARS IN DETAIL

Ralph reported the next week that he had been slightly relieved since going home to live with his mother, and although still in a state of constant tension had not been having panic attacks. He said that he was now aware through reading the chapters that panic attacks would not cause him any harm. He felt on reflection that he had been in a state of constant tension or mild panic before, but had developed ways to avoid having a full-blown panic attack.

Most of our second session was taken up in trying to understand his feelings a little more.

He described his symptoms as the need to go to the toilet, a quickening of his pulse, palpitations, extreme tension in the forehead, cold hands, shaking – all of which happened at the same time. Typical triggers were being alone in crowded shopping areas or pubs, or in queues and being alone driving the car.

His ultimate fear was that in a full-blown panic the tension would cause the chemical balance in his mind to alter his personality. He described the "powers of reasoning" as being "finely balanced", and an overload of anxiety might "make it go". He also thought the "overload" of anxiety would make him dizzy and tense, and eventually make him urinate and pass out. He summarized this as a fear of "losing control of the mind and body".

His safety routines were as follows:

- Avoiding crowded situations.

- Being able to leave the pub at any time.

- Withdrawing from any stressful situations.

- When going to the hairdresser, picking a particularly good moment or having a drink beforehand.

- When in a library, concentrating on the books to stop thinking about fear.

- Avoiding picking up cups when other people were present.

- When having to write on a blackboard, having a drink beforehand.

- Trying to exhaust himself physically before attempting things.

- Cutting down on tea.

- Finding a public toilet every so often to check his underwear to see if he had urinated.

His lifesavers were the following:

- On a particular day when he thought he would have a panic attack, he took a change of clothes with him (for fear of urination).

- When shaking, he would try to keep himself perfectly still.

- He would tell himself, "When I finally go crazy, I won't know about it and that will be OK."

- He would mentally resign himself to a life of disability.

I explained to him that by carrying out these routines he never really allowed himself to discover what would actually happen during a panic attack. He would always continue to believe that "anxiety overload" could lead to him losing control of his mind and body because the safety routines he employed stopped panic attacks occurring Even if they did start to occur he had lifesaving routines to reduce them, so he constantly shielded himself from knowing what would really happen. I explained that he needed to go into the sort of situations that might set off a panic attack without "withdrawing", as he put it.

SESSION 3: THE "CRUNCH POINT"

Ralph returned one week later. He was still living with his mother and did not feel as isolated as before. He was also sleeping better. He had been holding on to the idea that panic attacks pass of their own accord, as I had explained in the previous session. He had tried in a limited way to test this out by going into supermarkets for a short time.

Session 3 was to be our first real-life "exposure session". We would carry out exercises in town rather than spend the session in the office. I explained to Ralph again that it was important for him to try to set off a panic attack and "sweat it out" without withdrawing, so that he could discover what would really happen. We had already established that large stores were most likely to set off a panic attack, so I suggested to Ralph that we should go into Aberdeen city centre to a large store. Like most clients, this was the "crunch point" he most feared, but I think Ralph appreciated that he could not move forward much more without attempting this hurdle.

So we both set off in my car to the city centre, where we parked and walked down to Debenhams. In Aberdeen, Debenhams is in a covered mall and has three storeys. We started at the bottom floor: perfumes, jewellery, men's clothes and sportswear. Although Ralph felt fear and dread, he was interested in the men's clothing section – panic had for the last two years reduced his shopping to clothes you could buy in the village shop, or what relatives happened to buy for him. As we walked round together a short wave of panic hit him but soon passed.

I must seem like a pest at times like this to clients because I am always saying, "Did the attack pass off of its own accord or did you do something to bring it down?" exposing the little tricks and lifesavers that they are using to try to stifle a full panic attack. Well, yes, he was holding himself tense to avoid a panic attack getting worse. I again explained how he must allow the panic to come without trying to stop it in any way, so he was to stop purposely tensing himself.

We next went up the escalator to the first floor. Again we strolled round together but as most of it was women's clothing we decided to progress to the top floor. I asked Ralph to wander around this floor by himself and we agreed to meet at the top of the escalator five minutes later. When we met up, he explained that he had had a small peak of panic at first, but this had subsided. I then asked him to spend a further twenty minutes by himself on this floor before we met up again. He achieved this satisfactorily – he had felt on edge most of this time but no panic. We then went into the self-service café for a coffee, to review what he had achieved in this session and to help plan out "exercises" that he might carry out by himself before the next session. This may sound a pleasant end to the session, but going into a café had its own dreads, such as queuing and being trapped by having to sit at a table and finish your drink or meal. We were both very pleased with Ralph's achievements. His self-confidence was higher and, as I was to discover in the next session, he was already beginning to plan his own campaign on panic.

SESSION 4: PROGRESS!

Ralph returned a week later. He had gone into a supermarket himself and had a full-blown panic attack that reached its natural peak, then declined. During this, he said he was unaware of his surroundings and felt exhausted and defeated afterwards. He had expected a revelation but just felt defeat. However, over the next few days he had put his experience into perspective.

Later he pushed himself to do the week's shopping, again in the supermarket. He refused to leave the supermarket until he had got all the items on his shopping list, which in effect "trapped him" for a period of twenty minutes or so.

He had gone to a football match in Elgin, and he felt awful during the first half but OK in the second (Elgin United: 4; Huntly Football Club: 1). He had also driven forty miles by himself (for the first time) to our session in Aberdeen that day. Previously he had thought that forcing himself to have a panic attack would be some sort of magic drug, but he now saw that this was an over-exaggerated view and that overcoming panic would take time and persistence.

In this session, we reviewed these exercises he had described and his reactions to them, and made further plans. In my opinion, what Ralph had attempted in one week showed extreme bravery!

SESSION 5: COME ON, PANIC – LET'S GET IT OVER WITH!

Another week went by, and when Ralph returned for this session his list of successes included going to the supermarket, to the library, to a football match, to a huge shopping centre in Dundee, and spending three hours in a crowded restaurant.

He had stayed in these places until panic feelings had declined before leaving. He was now feeling much more positive and more willing to try things. Now, on good days, he felt calm throughout the day with only an occasional twinge of panic.

His worst test had been in the local library, where he felt a strong panic attack coming on, and he said to himself, "Come on; let's get it over with." He now felt that the best exercises were the hardest ones – they helped to confirm to him that the problem was on the way out. He felt that the therapy was helping him not to look inwards.

■ BEING ALONE

Ralph was beginning to think that he would almost have to reintroduce himself to society. He had noticed that panic attacks were most likely when he went into a new environment or had to do things alone, without support.

At this point, we spent quite a time discussing what "being alone" meant to Ralph. What happened in the session was that we were going back to discovering causes (as discussed in Chapters 9 and 10) rather than focusing on practical exercises to overcome his fear of panic.

To Ralph, "being alone" signified being unloved. He explained that before he was thirteen, supplies of love were a bit thin in his family. His mother had not shown him much affection and he had always felt a little detached from his parents. When his parents were discussing sending him to boarding school, he had said to them that he would rather be with them and their friends and have a poorer education. "But I always got the impression that they weren't listening."

At school, when he was alone he had felt that his parents couldn't love him if they did this to him and that "if *they* didn't love me I would never know real love in my life and never be able to sustain a relationship".

SESSIONS 6 TO 8: NOW THAT PANIC HAS GONE...

The first five sessions could be described as "core therapy" sessions. From then on, the sessions took a slightly different form. They now consisted of the following:

- Reviewing practical tasks that Ralph had carried out by himself, and deciding what the next steps should be.

- Reminding him of certain basic principles such as cutting out safety routines, the normality of good and bad days and the normality of fear sensations.

- Discussing in greater detail the causes for this panic, both in terms of events and in his own attitudes and approach.

- General discussions about his tendency to be pessimistic and negative. His thoughts included, "If I don't feel better after this therapy, I am never going to rid myself of this condition," and, "I am dependent on the sessions. When they go, I won't be able to rid myself of negative thoughts."

- Discussion on whether he really was a normal person or whether he had some mental weakness.

- More discussion on the significance of being alone, "being alienated" and the need for security.

- Discussion about his feelings of self-worth. This connected with being alone. At the back of his mind, he had thought, "When I am alone, I am unloved. If I am unloved, it is because I am unlovable. Therefore I am not a very nice person."

By Session 8, he no longer believed he would lose control and was not experiencing much anxiety in places that had previously bothered him. He said he felt he had previously spent so much time being afraid of what was going on in his own body that he had not learned how to deal with external fears. He also pinpointed the fact that fear had loomed so large in his life that other feelings had been shut off or stunted and he needed more time for his emotional life to grow. He needed to develop "emotional strength".

The significant breakthrough was that he had decided the time was right to go back to his cottage and live alone. He did this gradually from this session onwards.

SESSION 9: GOING BACK TO THE SCENE OF THE CRIME

Ralph explained how difficult it had been for him to go back to "the place where I thought I was going crazy". There were so many associations with the temptation to think "I'm going crazy" and, for instance, throw himself out of the window. But, he said, "I hold on to the idea it is not craziness, just anxiety."

SESSIONS 10 TO 12: CAN FEARS BE FORGOTTEN?

By Session 10, Ralph was coping quite well with living at home, and by Session 11, he had "almost forgotten" about being anxious in crowded shopping areas. He did experience some tension or anxiety in certain situations and had good days and bad days, but by and large was reasonably calm. These last few sessions were taken up with discussing his life in general, how he could handle relationships better, where he was going in life and what sort of job he might aim for. Previously he had not shared feelings much with others, for instance his parents or teachers at school. Now he said that his relationship with his mother had improved a lot, that he was able to share some of his difficulties and problems with her, and to his surprise she had listened and was understanding.

SESSION 13: CUTTING THE LAST THREAD

In this our last session, Ralph said that the panic had "almost entirely disappeared". He sometimes woke in the night thinking, "Where am I going in life?" But he had decided just to leave things to fate and see how they worked out for him. "I am not worrying about the future," he stated. One of the last things Ralph explained to me in this session was that he felt he should cut the threads with me – our sessions were a source of security for him, and he thought that now was the time to branch out by himself. Though it is sad to say goodbye to a client, this showed me how strong and healthy Ralph's attitude to life had now become.

16

SETTING UP YOUR OWN PERSONAL EXPERIMENT

Let's go through setting up a series of personal experiments in more detail; the nuts and bolts of facing fear. Here are some steps that panic sufferers could follow to test out what really happens in a panic:

- List the main situations or events that are most difficult or tend to make them panic. The list might look like this:

    1. Crowds, especially in big stores.
    2. Queuing.
    3. Being in a store and not being able to see the exit.
    4. Sitting relaxing in the evening.
    5. Running up the stairs.

- List the safety routines for each of these events – in other words what they do to stop panic happening. For example:

1. CROWDS
Take a Valium before I go out.
Take a friend with me.
Avoid big stores – go to smaller shops.
Go during weekdays when the crowds are smaller.
Only decide to go on the spur of the moment.
Only go on good days.

2. QUEUING
Don't use supermarkets.
Pick the smallest queue.
Only buy a few items of shopping.

3. BEING IN A STORE WITHOUT SEEING THE EXIT
Always make sure I know where the exit is before I go in.
Avoid stores where I might get "trapped".
Stay near the exit.
Keep checking to make sure I can always see the exit.
Make sure I can always see my friend/partner.

4. SITTING RELAXING IN THE EVENING
Always keep busy.
Try to keep my mind active with other things to distract me.
Don't watch the television for too long.
Always keep myself tense.
Don't watch exciting programmes, violence or topics about
   mental disorder.

5. RUNNING UP THE STAIRS
Never exert myself too quickly.
Creep up the stairs.
Arrange not to go upstairs too often.

- List the lifesavers – in other words all those things they do,
  once a panic starts, to bring it down, such as:

  taking a deep breath;
  trying to relax;
  telling myself, "You'll be OK, you'll be OK";
  taking a tablet;
  trying to find a chair to sit down on;
  lying down on the bed;
  finding a wall to lean against;
  starting to run;
  slapping myself;
  shaking my head from side to side;
  calling the doctor or a trusted friend;
  drinking water;
  drinking alcohol;
  trying to distract myself by reading or doing mental
     arithmetic.

In order to conduct a personal experiement the person must:

* go into feared situations, such as crowds;

* go without safety routines, such as taking Valium;

* go without lifesavers, such as taking a deep breath if panic starts.

Figure 13: A sliding scale to measure anxiety

perfectly relaxed		a bit tense		quite worked up		unpleasantly tense		very tense and panicky		terror and panic
0	1	2	3	4	5	6	7	8	9	10

Sufferers would probably find it helpful to keep a "Personal Experiments" log – a diary of what they achieved and what happened to them. This may include using a scoring system for anxiety feelings along a sliding scale (Figure 13, above) and a similar system from 0 to 10 indicating how much they believe harm will come to them during a panic (see Figure 14, below).

Figure 14: A sliding scale to measure belief in the danger of panic

completely safe		mostly safe		a bit dangerous		somewhat dangerous		dangerous		very dangerous
0	1	2	3	4	5	6	7	8	9	10

Every time sufferers try a new activity they give it a score, which they can record in their Personal Experiments log. This way they know whether anxiety sensations are improving or not, and whether their beliefs about panic ("appraisals") are changing.

ONE STEP AFTER ANOTHER

Some people are prepared to "get stuck in" and face their worst fear straight away, once they understand how important it is. Others are more cautious. They may need to have a friend or relative with them for support at first. If so, they should make sure the friend reads this book so that they have an understanding of panic. Usually there is a whole series of experiments that the person needs to carry out.

Based on the example above, the sufferer might want to test something more manageable at first, like sitting relaxing in the evening. As the first experiment they might plan to sit watching television for an hour without distracting themselves, jumping up or keeping busy doing other things. At this stage, they might feel they need to choose a "safe" TV programme (not violent or about mental illness). In future experiments, they may wish to choose a difficult programme or just watch television without knowing what will be shown.

■ **WHAT WOULD A SUFFERER FIND OUT AFTER THIS FIRST EXPERIMENT?**

Did they panic? If they did, were they able to see it through to the end? What did they learn? What remains to be tested out? For their second experiment, they may decide to do exactly the same thing again. They may have felt that the results were a fluke and need to find out if the same happens again. After this experiment, their confidence may be rising, and they may want to make the experiment a bit more risky. They may purposely pick a violent film and plan to see it through to the end (I am talking about the usual police films or cowboy stuff, not heavy violence).

After this, they may feel that they can cope with panic at home, but are less certain about what might happen outside. They still need to carry out many mini-experiments with watching television (for example, in the afternoon, in the late evening, by themselves, in a group, different sorts of film) and consolidate on those first experiments. But the next key experiments should be outside the home. They may try supermarkets, and later queuing in supermarkets. Later still they may try doing this on bad days. Throughout the experiments they will probably realize the extent to which they had previously tried to "cushion" themselves from a panic, and hopefully they will begin to drop all their attempts at suppressing and controlling panic. Usually, as in Ralph's case, a person needs to carry out a whole series of personal experiments to test out the many details of their fears.

FOUR KEY PRINCIPLES FOR A SOUND PROGRAMME OF EXPERIMENTS

■ THE MAIN OBJECT OF THE EXPERIMENTS IS TO HAVE A PANIC ATTACK

If sufferers go through the experiments without ever panicking, what have they learned? They may have learned something useful – that panic is less frequent than they thought – and it may encourage them a lot. But there is a hidden snare. Very quietly and automatically the goal of therapy begins to change and when they finally do panic they feel devastated and deflated. All that has gone wrong is they have defined success as "no panic", whereas the real success is having and facing a panic. If someone goes through therapy without a panic, all may be well for the future; but the likelihood is that at some time in the future they will have a panic or mini-panic and be unable to deal with it. Learning about panic first-hand is the best immunization programme for the future.

■ FACING THE THING A PERSON FEARS MOST WILL BE UNPLEASANT, EVEN TERRIFYING

The sufferer will experience great discomfort, anxiety and fear. It takes a lot of courage. When they are changing their usual routine and facing the monster of fear, they will often get worse at first, more agitated and exhausted. This is to be expected because they are pushing themselves rather than running from fear. But after this period of strain – if they are able to face their very worst fear – they will discover that there is no reality behind the fear and they will be on their way to recovery. In other words, with this approach the person can expect to get worse before getting better. The experience might be labelled "unpleasant but safe".

■ EACH EXPERIMENT MUST BE GIVEN ENOUGH TIME
A few minutes of watching television or being in crowds will not usually teach sufferers much about panic. They must continue the experiment until they feel they have discovered what they had intended to discover. Forty-five minutes is a good yardstick to have in mind for any exercise. Sometimes having to stay for a fixed amount of time means that they are "trapped" enough to set off panic, whereas being able to escape from difficult situations at any time may be enough to stop a panic attack ever happening. So a fixed time is usually a good idea. It is amazing how something terrifying can lose its power with sufficient time. Sometimes the real power of the fear slips away without the person knowing the exact time of its departure. Some previously feared activities actually become boring after a while.

Sufferers should never attempt to leave a situation when anxiety is high or mounting – this may make the problem worse. They should try to leave after anxiety has passed its peak or when anxiety is not very high.

■ CHOOSING THE NEXT PERSONAL EXPERIMENT
After each experiment, the person should ask, "What do I still need to do to convince myself that panic is safe?" or, "Deep down, what do I still feel is dangerous about having a panic attack?" The answers can be used to guide future experiments. It is quite common for people to carry out their personal experiments on good days. What do they learn? They learn they can cope on good days, but they still feel very uneasy about doing tasks on bad days. Would something awful happen on those days when dread and depression are so close at hand? This is the clue for the next experiment – purposely doing the same tasks on bad days. If the person can discover that even then panic is safe, this really helps to dismantle bad days. They occur less often.

People vary in the pace they can take the experiments – one person, like Terry, may do the most risky experiment first, whereas others prefer to increase the risk factor only little by little. That's OK if they are learning something new about panic each time.

PART V

THE PANIC SUFFERER AS NORMAL

17

CURES, HALF-CURES, AND LIMITATIONS

Why should someone go through all the pain and anxiety of these personal experiments? To be worthwhile the sufferer has to press in on those very things they are most afraid of – and that is agonizing at times. But is it worth it?

WHY BOTHER?

These are the typical benefits of the therapy:

- Panic attacks will occur less often.

- Panic attacks will be far less severe.

- Even if the odd panic occurs in the future, the person will feel uncomfortable but not afraid.

- The person will feel more relaxed and won't have to fight off impending panics or struggle to control panic.

- The amazing clutter of avoidance behaviour, safety routines, and lifesavers will start to disappear.

- The person's mood will lift. They will feel less generally anxious and depressed, and they will feel less dread.

- The person will not need to depend on tranquillizers or take antidepressants.

- The person will be able to get on with their life and personal development rather than being locked into a prison of fear (though note that recovery may affect the balance of relationships – others may have to adapt to a less dependent person).

- The person's social, work, sex, and leisure life should be much freer.

WHAT IF I CANNOT FACE PERSONAL EXPERIMENTS?

This is entirely up to the discretion of an individual. Everyone is different, and what suits one may not suit another. For many individuals, simply knowing the facts about panic seems to be all they need. Others need to prove it to themselves.

It may be that the person is just too fearful to attempt any experiments or is not convinced they are necessary. In this case, it may be better not to try. Some try and have to give up – they certainly should not feel that is a failure.

Often people need the strong support of others to get through these experiments. Very often the guiding knowledge and support of a therapist is necessary. For some sufferers, a self-help book is just not enough. What are they to do? They probably need the individual guidance and help of a clinical psychologist or cognitive-behavioural therapist, or they may want some medication to help them. They should go to their own doctor for advice in the first instance, to discover the options available. The amount of experience therapists have with panic sufferers may vary greatly, so it is best to get as much advice as possible about their experience and the sort of approach they would provide (some useful contacts are provided in the reference section at the end of this book).

In their first session the therapist or an assistant will interview them in some depth and try to understand the problem in detail. They should then discuss the best way forward with the patient. They may well be able to identify why the person is not succeeding with the approach in this book and will present their own solutions for overcoming the problem. There is variation from one therapist to another and they may well use a different approach from mine. There are also many other advantages to talking to someone face to face. Sometimes the relief in talking to someone who understands the problem is very helpful.

There are also a number of self-help groups for panic and anxiety sufferers, often run on a voluntary basis by the sufferers themselves. They are often useful in helping the person realize that they are not alone in their suffering, and in providing support and care from those who understand (see the reference list at the back of this book).

The sufferer is the best judge of whether to attempt these exercises and there should be no sense of shame or failure for someone who does not want to do them. Everyone's individual circumstances are different and we are talking about a serious and powerful enemy – fear – which is not to be underestimated.

WHEN SHOULD PERSONAL EXPERIMENTS NOT BE DONE?

There are cases where an experiment should not be done. The obvious ones are those in which the person has a known diagnosed condition, such as a heart condition or asthma, in which exertion or strain makes them worse. If an asthmatic person does a personal experiment, it may have the reverse effect – rather than showing how safe panic is, it may show how dangerous it is. The guiding principle should be: if in doubt consult your doctor about what to do.

WHEN SHOULD A PERSON STOP DOING PERSONAL EXPERIMENTS?

The simple answer is: when they have discovered what they need to know about panic. There is no need to keep experiments going for months and months. An upper limit for a series of experiments would be about four months. They are for the purpose of discovery. Once someone has discovered the facts about their panic anxiety, there's no need to keep going on and on. Certainly experiments should not become a way of life; rather, they should be one stage of life that can later be forgotten.

HOW FAR CAN RECOVERY GO?

A full recovery is possible. But what do we mean by "a full recovery"? It does *not* mean that the person will be 100 per cent free of panic attacks. If 100 per cent freedom is the goal of therapy, then there is a problem – it probably means that the person is still afraid of panics. With a full recovery, the person is no longer afraid of panic attacks, and not thrown if they should have the occasional panic. They may experience panic and anxiety from time to time if they are going through periods of stress and difficulty. It would be normal to expect that. However, if the person is not afraid of this and realizes that they are not "slipping back", any panicky phase should not last too long; it is unpleasant but not threatening. Over a longer period of time panics may disappear altogether.

WHAT IF I'VE DONE EVERYTHING THE BOOK SAYS AND AM NO BETTER?

If, after carefully following the ideas in this book, a sufferer is not improving, they should stop "bashing their head against a brick wall" and discontinue the exercises. But remember:

- The person must really put their fear of dying, going mad, or whatever it may be to the test. If they keep avoiding it, even with clever tricks, they have not really done the exercises properly – and cannot expect a full recovery.

- The person must continue with the approach for long enough to really find out what happens. Dipping a toe in the water just won't work. For instance, if someone goes into crowds once and leaves it at that, they have not given the experiment a full enough test.

- If the person does all the exercises but never has a panic attack they may realize that the activities are safe enough, but they have not discovered that panic attacks are also safe. If in the future they never panic again, all may be well. On the other hand, if they do happen to have a panic, they will be thrown. So it is the panic attack that must be faced, not the activities or places that set off a panic.

- When sufferers try to set off a panic attack – let's say by going into crowds – they must stay long enough for the panic to happen and then to subside. Five minutes will not usually be enough – it is more like an hour that is needed.

- Patience is required – the person cannot expect an overnight cure. I have heard it said that it takes the same amount of time to get over a stress problem as it took to develop. I don't know about that – it certainly isn't scientifically proved – but it is right in the sense that the idea of an immediate wonder cure is a snare to the sufferer.

- The person should not let a setback make them think that the approach is failing. Setbacks are normal. There *will* be setbacks. They do *not* spell failure.

If after carrying out all this advice there is no obvious improvement, it is time to stop.

18

LET'S FINISH OFF PANIC

In this chapter, I would like to draw the main points of this book together.

- A panic attack is the body's normal fear reaction. Everyone has the potential for a fear reaction. Usually the fear reaction is switched on when danger comes along. It is there to help us escape quickly from the danger. In the first few attacks of the panic sufferer, the fear reaction is switched on *by accident*.

- But sufferers don't know that. They think that because the feelings of the fear reaction are so strong, something really serious must be happening to them.

- A time of stress or crisis, or a series of changes in the sufferer's life usually occurs in the nine months before their first panic.

- Because the person ignores the signs of stress and does nothing to resolve the situation, pressure builds to bursting point.

- Under this pressure, the fear reaction is accidentally switched on or triggered. Alternatively, some drugs such as cannabis can trigger off the fear reaction.

- Sufferers do not make the connection between their life stress and the first panic attacks.

- Not knowing the real cause of the panics, a sufferer becomes very afraid of more attacks and what might happen to them during the attacks.

- This fear changes them. They begin to become oversensitive to any feelings resembling panic, to look inwards too much, to try to find ways to stop panic happening or neutralize it when it starts.

- The effort to avoid panic clutters up and changes the person's life. They spend far too much time and energy taking precautions and evading panic feelings.

- Sufferers are basically the same as they ever were but are so caught up by fear that they seem to change. However, once they understand what is happening to them and lose their fear of panic, they can get back to normal.

THE CONTRIBUTION OF THIS BOOK

This book has been arranged in five sections. The first provides a basic explanation about panic. The second covers some of the typical mistaken ideas people have about panic and the third looks at how to identify causes for panic. The fourth section describes how to test out what really happens in panic by using personal experiments. The fourth section is the practical back-up to the earlier chapters concerning mistaken ideas, but instead of being informed by others of the facts, the sufferer is encouraged to discover the truth through their own personal experience.

WHY PANIC SUFFERERS ARE NORMAL

The panic sufferer does not have any mental aberrations or illness, but is a normal individual, because:

- the first panics have a definite and logical cause (crisis/ stress);

- the person's way of emotionally handling stressful events may be less than ideal, but emotional processing style is learned from our families and is not an illness;

- the fear reaction (which is the same as a panic attack) is common to everyone;

- the reason panics can continue over a long period of time

involves the sufferer's lack of understanding about panics and mistaken ideas that cause them to avoid panic;

- the strength of the sufferer's fear about what others may call harmless (for example, crowds or palpitations) is entirely reasonable given their mistaken ideas about panic being dangerous. They are reacting to danger just as a person should do.

The main culprit is the sufferer's mistaken idea about the danger of panic. This can be corrected by:

- accurate information;
- personal "corrective" experience;
- understanding emotions better.

RESTORING AND REBUILDING

Although for the sufferer panics appear completely bewildering and illogical, once they begin to understand the fear reaction it all makes sense. There is much suffering involved in panic; the panic sufferer's life revolves around panic and fear. It is possible to overcome this and return from that terrifying orbit around fear to being able to concentrate on normal everyday life, but when this happens the person will have some catching up to do. The years of concentration on panic often means that the sufferer has missed out on so many of the ordinary things in life. Fortunately, their problem does not permanently damage their mental faculties, which are untouched through the worst panic experience. Concentration, memory, feeling at ease – none of this is permanently lost, only temporarily suppressed by fear, and all this can return. If you are a panic sufferer yourself, I hope it *does* return for you.

THE SUBJECT MATTER CATCHES UP WITH THE AUTHOR

A strange thing happened during the writing of this book. I had started off writing for those who suffer from panic – I had some feeling for them and an understanding of what they were going through, but despite my knowledge of their condition, I was basically writing for "them", the sufferers. However, during the course of writing this book, I too became one of "them". For the first time in my life, I experienced an anxiety and panic disturbance that took me about nine months to get over. I was reluctant to mention my own account in this book at first but decided it might help others in their struggle with panic.

The whole thing caught me unawares. Looking back I should have seen it coming. You would expect a clinical psychologist to be able to spot the warning signs in himself! But I didn't. I did realize I was under stress, but assumed it would blow over and things would get back to normal again.

A NIGHT I'D RATHER FORGET

One night shortly after going to bed my physiological system seemed to go into a different gear. Instead of my body slowing down and quickly dropping off to sleep (the normal routine), everything seemed to be speeding up – heartbeat, sweating, tension, breathing.

At first I didn't worry, simply saying to myself, "Relax – it will pass, as usual." But after several attempts to go to sleep my whole system was still racing and getting faster, not slower. It doesn't sound so very fantastic or particularly scary as I tell it now, but as my attempts to shrug it off failed, I began to get concerned. I woke my wife to talk. I went downstairs to heat some milk. I tried some aspirin – but was still sweating, getting hotter, really tense. I was not able to breathe properly, and my heart was racing.

I suppose one advantage of being a psychologist was that I instantly identified it as anxiety, not some physical disorder, but that didn't stop it happening. I went back to bed, but I was tossing and turning a lot, so decided to go down to the lounge to set up a makeshift bed there. After watching a bit of late-night television, hoping to distract myself, and after yet more hot milk, I tried again to sleep. This would have been about two to three hours after the attack started. Still everything was twice as fast as normal.

FEAR STEPS IN

Somewhere around this stage, after all my efforts to calm down had failed, fear seemed to step in. Looking back now, the event is organized in my mind, and I am presenting a much clearer picture of what happened. At the time, it was unclear, chaotic and very, very unpleasant. Many of the fears related to the future. They were all of a type we could call "supposing" fears:

- "Supposing" my body carried on at this rate, I could never get to sleep. I couldn't do my job properly. I would lose my job, be made redundant, not be able to support my family.

- "Supposing" my body carried on at this rate, I would be continuously aware of my heartbeat and breathing and not be able to concentrate on the more detailed things one needs to do as a clinical psychologist – such as listening carefully to patients, picking up clues from what they said, working out what to focus on next in the session, giving a lecture or writing an article.

- "Supposing" I was continuously aware of heartbeat and breathing, I would have no peace and be in constant misery.

Over the next few days I continued at work, though not giving my best to patients – the feeling of dread and intrusive awareness of unpleasant bodily sensations made it quite difficult to concentrate on the sessions. I remember on the Friday there was an annual local meeting of psychologists, and I had to give a brief presentation about research. I was sweating profusely and tending to pant and sigh a lot, but tried to cover this up in the presentation. I wonder if any of my colleagues noticed my distress.

BEYOND NORMAL EXPERIENCE

At an early stage, I recalled the comment panic sufferers had often made, that it was impossible for others to understand how painful the experience was for them. I could now understand what they were talking about. The general mood I experienced was one of pervasive dread and fear of staying like this, followed after a few weeks by a longer depressed period in which I lost my sense of purpose in life. I slept little over the months. It struck me once or twice that this experience was like my idea of hell. Previous experiences of "normal" anxiety, such as exams, visiting the dentist or having to give a speech, simply did not equip me to understand what was happening now. I seemed to have entered a sort of different mood-world that was qualitatively different from anything I had experienced before.

WEATHERING THE STORM

In that first week, when I was at a low ebb, the parable that Jesus told about a wise man building his house on rock came to mind. When the wind and rains came and beat down, the house on the rock stood firm. Although I felt appalling and my emotions were about as far from "peace" as can be imagined, surprisingly my faith in God stayed firm. I was able to pray to him (which I did more than usual!) and hear from him as well as I did normally. Any closeness or reality was all now, *in the present*; I had no hope for recovery in the future, no sense or promise that I would ever get out of this.

The experience was as close to a solid rock in the midst of storms as any other analogy I can think of. Something quite central in my life was remaining stable while other things were falling to pieces, and this was important to my eventual recovery.

RED-HOT COALS

A firm understanding of panic and anxiety symptoms was ingrained in me when my own problem started. I had regularly explained panic symptoms to patients and had spent hours reading about them and thinking about them for this book. Knowing what was happening – what the sensations were – and particularly knowing that no harm such as madness or heart attack could come of them was a tremendous benefit. It probably reduced my symptoms from the very start. This has reinforced my belief that correct understanding of panic attacks is very important. The problem did seem to seek out areas where my knowledge was a bit weak, but I did some "revision", which eventually helped.

Technically, what I experienced were not full-blown panic attacks, but could be described as "limited panic attacks" – only certain symptoms occurred and they did not rise to a climax like a panic attack. The problem was closer to a more continuous over-awareness of bodily sensations.

I spent a great deal of time trying to reason myself out of sensations or persuade myself they were safe. An important part of recovery was to regard thoughts/awareness of bodily sensations as red-hot coals that I had to "drop" as soon as they came to mind rather than dwelling on them. Over the months this meant that I became less self-absorbed.

SO WHAT?

A breakthrough occurred one Sunday, after my wife and I had been for a walk with a couple who are our close friends. As we walked I tried to explain to the husband how the problem was really disrupting my life and how I felt as if I were under a cloud of moderate dread or fear so often now. Later in the afternoon, when we had returned home, an idea came to me that was a bit like a "eureka" feeling. The idea is not so very surprising, and I am sure I'd thought it several times before without it having any impact on me at all. But this time it really did "click": "If I am aware of my heart rate and breathing – *so what?*" From that point, I put into operation all the exercises about facing fear described in this book. Before, I had been trying to avoid awareness of certain bodily sensations. Now I tried to increase them. I said the words "heart rate" aloud several times. I kept purposely thinking of the things I had previously feared and avoided. I pondered how to purposely increase these sensations, and hit on the idea of jogging. I regularly jogged from then on.

PLODDING ON

Things progressed from this point – not necessarily smoothly, but they progressed. After about eight months, I reached the point where I had forgotten for most of the day that there was a problem. In my recovery, some words of the author Claire Weekes had been percolating in my mind ever since I had written a review chapter on an article she had written, called "The Key to Resisting Relapse in Panic".[1] These words proved helpful, and encouraged me to persist in adopting the right attitude whenever a setback occurred:

"Memory is always capable of recalling nervous symptoms, and what a heyday an anxious inner voice has then. It says 'It's all back again! Every lock, stock and barrel. Every member of the family! We're all here. What are you going to do now? You'll never recover now, you know!' What power the wrong voice holds. But if the right learned voice is there it will come to the rescue and say, 'You've been here before, you know the way!' Then, in spite of being possibly shocked and temporarily thrown off balance, the owner of that inner voice does know what to do and gradually does it."

Have the problems disappeared? Certain bodily sensations or moods such as tension, lack of concentration and increased heart rate do still occur when I am overworked or stressed in some way. That's only to be expected. But what is now missing is fear – fear of these feelings. And what a difference that makes.

POSTSCRIPT TO THE THIRD EDITION

Since the first edition of this book in 1995, many people have written to me, often saying how useful they found my own account of panic. And I nearly didn't put it into the original version! It has now been twenty years since I went through that experience and in retrospect some things have become a little clearer since I wrote it. I thought it might be helpful to briefly add them to this chapter.

FEAR OF...

Claire Weekes' words quoted above have proved so true for me: "If the right learned voice is there it will come to the rescue and say, 'You've been here before, you know the way.'" From time to time I experienced increased symptoms of stress or temporarily got bogged down with the same problems. Remembering back to how bad it was at the time, how long it had continued and how hope had nearly faded, was in a way comforting. I reasoned that if I had moved from that state to one where I mostly forgot there was a problem it meant that despite the temporary distress, it was likely the same would happen again. By doing what had proved successful before, it would be successful again. Claire Weekes, I found, had hit the nail on the head. I've begun to refer to this as "Fear of...". That is, the realization that the object feared is not the problem – chest pains, palpitations, racing thoughts, or whatever – it is the *fear of* that object that is the problem. This is not a startling revelation, because many people have identified that it is fear itself that is the real issue:

"The only thing we have to fear is fear itself."
Franklin D. Roosevelt

"If a man harbours any sort of fear, it makes him landlord to a ghost."
Lloyd Douglas

"The only thing I am afraid of is fear."
Arthur Wellesley, Duke of Wellington

"Nothing in life is to be feared. It is only to be understood."
Marie Curie

Even though this is a well-trodden path, it is good to find out from our own personal experience. Fear is the oxygen that keeps the flames alight; remove the oxygen and the flames wither. Progressively I have learned to recognize "fear of…" pretty quickly and to take my gaze off the thing feared.

A GREATER UNDERSTANDING OF ROOT CAUSES

In Chapters 9 to 11 we have explored the role of unidentified emotional stresses in the development of the first panic attack. Chapter 9 also outlines some research studies suggesting that just before the first panic attack, there is also a period of lowered resistance. In hindsight, over the years I have realized a few connections that were not completely clear when I first wrote the account of my experience. They became clearer to me after I had moved to a new job in the south of England. When the panic started, I had been living in Aberdeen for about thirteen years. Aberdeen is in the far north of Scotland, and it took one or two days' travelling to visit our families in England. Aberdeen is a self-sufficient and in many ways vibrant city, but is somewhat isolated from the rest of the UK. I had been doing the same job for those thirteen years, making less contact with colleagues outside Scotland, and not going to conferences and meetings elsewhere, so in terms of family and work, I was progressively becoming cut off from my roots. I felt stale and was going nowhere. I had uncomfortably claustrophobic mental pictures of continuing to work and then retire in the same place. I was not aware of how stifled and trapped I felt. That was a sort of background – an unresolved issue.

Like Katy (who was described in chapter 10), I was only dimly aware of this and had not properly processed it, and, being unaware, I had not done anything to alleviate it. On the week before my first panic, I was certainly at the period of lowest resistance. In general I had overstretched myself and was seeing too many patients; the weekend before, I had offered counselling to a friend who came to stay at our house for the whole weekend, and, whereas my idea of counselling was one or two fifty-minute sessions, hers was a wall-to-wall therapy marathon. I don't think I've ever had a less "refreshing" weekend! In addition, I was scheduled to attend an intensive three-day course starting the next day about childhood sexual abuse, which I found disturbing. But like most people who experience sudden panic attacks, my whole attention was sucked into the attacks themselves, rather than these external sources of stress.

In retrospect I can see these things clearer now – had I talked to someone at the time (it's quite hard for a psychologist to own up to being in trouble), I might have identified this sooner. The move to the south of England opened up many new possibilities for me and put me closer to my cultural roots, giving me hope and a sort of greater background sense of ease. I hope you too find such a place of ease in your own life.

NOTES

Chapter 1

1. American Psychiatric Association, *Diagnostic and Statistical Manual of Mental Disorders*, fourth edition, text revision, Washington, DC: American Psychiatric Association, 2000.

2. In the UK, the government-backed IAPT scheme (Improving Access to Psychological Therapies) uses self-help books as a first step in therapy. *Understanding Panic Attacks* is consistent with the therapeutic ideas behind IAPT.

3. Baker, R. & McFadyen, M., "Cognitive Invalidation and the Enigma of Exposure", in E. Karas (ed.), *Current Issues in Clinical Psychology*, 2, New York: Plenum Press, 1985; McFadyen, M. "The Cognitive Invalidation Approach to Panic", Chapter 13 in R. Baker (ed.), *Panic Disorder: Theory, Research and Therapy*, Chichester: John Wiley, 1989.

4. Marks, I. M., "Exposure Treatments: Clinical Applications", in W. S. Agras (ed.), *Behaviour Modification Principles and Clinical Applications* (2nd edn), Boston: Little, Brown & Co., 1978; Blakey, R., Baker, R., "An exposure approach to alcohol abuse" in *Behaviour Research and Therapy*, 18, 1980, pp. 29–25.

5. Butt, T., *George Kelly: The Psychology of Personal Constructs*, Basingstoke: Palgrave Macmillan, 2008.

6. Beck, A. T., Emery, G. & Greenberg, R. L., *Anxiety Disorders and Phobias; A Cognitive Perspective*, New York: Basic Books, 1985; Clark, D. M. & Salkovskis, P. M., "Cognitive therapy for panic and hyperchondriasis", Oxford: Pergamon Press, 1989.

7. Rapee, R. M. & Barlow, D. H., "Psychological treatment of unexpected panic attacks: cognitive behavioural component", Chapter 11 in R. Baker (ed.) *Panic Disorder: Theory, Research and Therapy*, Chichester: John Wiley, 1989; Barlow, D. H., *Anxiety and It's Disorders; The Nature and Treatment of Anxiety and Panic*, New York: Guilford Press, 1988.

8. Baker, R. (ed.), *Panic Disorder: Theory, Research and Therapy*, Chichester: John Wiley, 1989.

9. Baker, R., "Personal Accounts of Panic", chapter 5 in R. Baker (ed.), *Panic Disorder: Theory, Research and Therapy*, Chichester: John Wiley, 1989.

10. McFayden, M., "The Cognitive Invalidation Approach to Panic",

Chapter 13, in R. Baker (ed.), *Panic Disorder: Theory, Research and Therapy*, Chichester: John Wiley, 1989; Kelly, G. A., *A Theory of Personality*, New York: Norton, 1963.

11. Baker, R., Holloway, J., Thomas, P., Thomas, S., & Owen, M., "Emotional Processing and Panic", *Behaviour Research and Therapy*, 42, 2004, pp. 271–87.

12. Baker, R., *Emotional Processing: Healing through Feeling*, Oxford: Lion, 2007; Baker, R. *Understanding Trauma: How to Overcome Post Traumatic Stress*, Oxford: Lion, 2010.

13. Sánchez-Meca, J., Rosa-Alcázar, A.I., Marín-Martínez, F., & Gómez-Conesa, "Psychological treatment of panic disorder with or without agoraphobia: A meta-analysis", *Clinical Psychology Review*, 30, 2010, pp. 37–50.

14. NICE clinical guidelines for the management of anxiety in adults in primary, secondary and community care. Guideline CG22, National Institute of Clinical Effectiveness, December 2004.

15. Baker, R., Nunn, J., & Sinclair, J., *A System for Evaluating the Effectiveness of Therapy*, Final Report of Clinical Audit Study to the Grampian Health Board, Aberdeen: Grampian Health Board, 1993.

Chapter 2

1. Kessler, R. C., Chiu, W. T., Jin. R., Ruscio, A. M., Shear, K., & Walters, E. E., "The Epidemiology of Panic Attacks, Panic Disorder and Agoraphobia in the National Comorbidity Survey Replication", *Archives of General Psychiatry*, 63, 2006, pp. 415–24.

2. Vose, R. H., *Agoraphobia*, London: Faber and Faber, 1981.

3. McKinnon, E., *In Stillness Conquer Fear*, Blackburn, Victoria: Dove Communications, 1983.

4. Freedman, R., "Ambulatory Monitoring Findings on Panic", Chapter 4 in R. Baker (ed.), *Panic Disorder: Theory, Research and Therapy*, Chichester: John Wiley, 1989.

5. Zane, M. D., "A Contextual Approach to Panic", Chapter 8 in R. Baker (ed.), *Panic Disorder: Theory, Research and Therapy*, Chichester: John Wiley, 1989.

6. Iancu, I., Levin, J., Dannon, P. N., Poreh, A., Ben-Yehuda, Y. & Kottler, M., "Prevalence of self reported phobia symptoms in an Israeli sample of young conscripts", *Journal of Anxiety Disorders*, 21, 2007, pp. 762–69.

Chapter 3

1. Raymond, E., *The Autobiography of David*, London: Victor Gollancz, 1946.

2. Vose, R. H., *Agoraphobia*, London: Faber and Faber, 1981.

Chapter 5

1. Basoglu, M., Marks, I.M. & Sengun, S., "A Prospective Study of Anxiety in Agoraphobia with Panic Disorder", *British Journal of Psychiatry*, 160, 1992, pp. 57–64; Kenardy, J., Fried, L., Kraemer, & Barr Taylor, C., "Psychological Precursors of Panic Attacks", *British Journal of Psychiatry*, 160, 1992, pp. 668–73; Waring, H., "The Nature of Panic Attack Symptoms", Chapter 2 in R. Baker (ed.), *Panic Disorder: Theory, Research and Therapy*, Chichester: John Wiley, 1989.

Chapter 6

1. Kezdi, P., *You and Your Heart: How to Take Care of Your Heart for a Long Healthy Life*, Harmondsworth: Penguin, 1981.

2. The normal blood pressure for a healthy adult varies a great deal, but generally should measure somewhere in the region of 120/80. If the reading is in excess of 150/90, it is classed as high blood pressure.

3. NICE clinical guidelines for the management of anxiety in adults in primary, secondary and community care. Guideline CG22, National Institute of Clinical Effectiveness, December 2004.

4. Huffman, J. C. & Pollack, M. H. "Predicting Panic Disorder Among Patients with Chest Pain: An Analysis of the Literature", *Psychosomatics*, 44, 2003, pp. 222–36.

5. Weekes, C., *Peace from Nervous Suffering*, London: Angus and Robertson, 1972.

6. Van Den Hout, M., De Jong, P., & Merchelbach, H., "On the Termination of Panic Attacks", *Behaviour Research and Therapy*, 31, 1993, pp. 117–18.

Chapter 8

1. Zane, M. D., "A Contextual Approach to Panic", Chapter 8 in R. Baker (ed.), *Panic Disorder: Theory, Research and Therapy*, Chichester: John Wiley, 1989.

Chapter 9

1. Clark, J. C. & Wardman, W., *Agoraphobia: A Clinical and Personal Account*, Sydney: Pergamon, 1985.
2. Hibbert, G. A., "Ideational Components of Anxiety: Their Origin and Content", *British Journal of Psychiatry*, 144, 1984, pp. 618–24.

Chapter 11

1. Baker, R., Holloway, J., Thomas, P., Thomas, S., & Owen, M., "Emotional Processing & Panic", *Behaviour Research and Therapy*, 42, 2004, pp. 271–87.
2. Rachman, S., "Emotional Processing", *Behaviour Research and Therapy*, 18, 1980, pp. 51–60.
3. Baker, R. *Emotional Processing: Healing through Feeling*, Oxford: Lion Hudson, 2007.
4. Barlow, D. H., "Unravelling the mysteries of anxiety and its disorders from the perspective of emotion theory", *American Psychologist*, November 2000, pp. 1247–63.
5. Plomin, R., De Fries, J. C., McLean, G. E. & Rutter, M. *Behavioural Genetics: A Primer* (3rd edn), New York: Freeman, 1997; Olaunji, B. O. & Wolitzky-Taylor, K. B. "Anxiety Sensitivity and the Anxiety Disorders: A Meta-Analytic Review and Synthesis", *Psychological Bulletin*, 135, 2009, pp. 974–99.
6. Clark, D. M., "Panic Disorder: from theory to therapy" in P. M. Salkovkis (ed.), *Frontiers of Cognitive Therapy*, New York: Guilford Press, 1996.
7. Fava, L. & Morton, J., "Causal modelling of panic disorder theories", *Clinical Psychology Review*, 29, 2009, pp. 623–37.
8. Lazarus, R. S., *Stress and Emotion: A New Synthesis*, London: Free Association Books, 1999.
9. Gendlin, E. T., *Focusing*, New York: Bantam Books, 1981.
10. Greenberg, L. & Safran, J. D., *Emotion in Psychotherapy*, New York: The Guildford Press, 1987.

Chapter 12

1. Mathews, A. M., Gelder, M. G., & Johnston, D. W., *Agoraphobia: Nature and Treatment*, London: Tavistock Publications, 1981.

Chapter 13

1. Spielberger, C. D., "Anxiety as an Emotional State", in C. D. Spielberger (ed.), *Anxiety: Current Trends in Theory and Research*, Vol. 1, New York: Academic Press, 1972.

Chapter 14

1. McFadyen, M., "The Cognitive Invalidation Approach to Panic", Chapter 13 in R. Baker (ed.), *Panic Disorder: Theory, Research and Therapy*, Chichester: John Wiley, 1989; Kelly, G. A., *A Theory of Personality*, New York: Norton, 1963.

Chapter 19

1. Weekes, C. & Baker, R. "The Key to Resisting Relapse in Panic", Chapter 15 in R. Baker (ed.), *Panic Disorder: Theory, Research and Therapy*, Chichester: John Wiley, 1989.

HELP FOR PANIC SUFFERERS

■ **SELF-HELP BOOKS**

Baker, R., *Emotional Processing: Healing through Feeling*, Oxford: Lion Hudson, 2007.

Weekes, C., *Self-Help for Your Nerves*, London: Thorsons, 1995.

Weekes, C., *Peace from Nervous Suffering*, London: Penguin Books Ltd, 1991.

Weekes, C., *More Help for Your Nerves*, London: Thorsons, 1995.

■ **INFORMATION WEBSITES**

www.anxietyuk.org.uk/index.php is run by the charity AnxietyUK, which was initially set up by people with experience of anxiety disorders. It offers a mixture of free information and a membership service that provides volunteer-run therapy options, a helpline, and online help.

www.emotionalprocessing.org.uk supplements this book and contains a wealth of information regarding emotional processing and many psychological problems, including panic attacks. It is the product of the author, Dr Roger Baker's clinical experience and his research team's findings.

www.nhs.uk/conditions/panic-disorder is a National Health Service website providing information on panic disorder. It describes the different types of anxiety and how panic disorder fits into it, the treatments available, information about medication, and self-help suggestions.

www.nomorepanic.co.uk is a website offering lots of free information for registered members. It has a forum through which sufferers and carers can support each other and share information.

www.nopanic.org.uk/index.html is the website of the No Panic charity. It has a dedicated support phone line staffed by volunteers and it also provides information and links to other resources.

www.topuk.org is the Triumph Over Phobias website and is, as the title implies, mainly for those with phobias. It provides information and updates of local support groups for phobias and OCD.

- **HELPLINE**

The No Panic organization has a free helpline: 0808 808 0545, or from outside the UK call +44 (0) 1952 590005. Alternatively, email ceo@nopanic.org.uk

INDEX

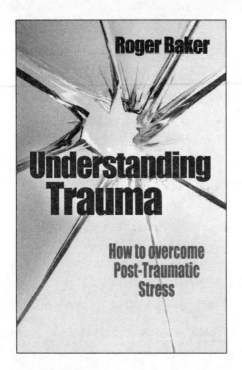

ALSO AVAILABLE FROM THE SAME AUTHOR

Understanding Trauma

In this title Dr Roger Baker explains the many symptoms of Post Traumatic Stress. Based on twenty years of research and clinical practice, he lays out a self-help programme – Emotional Processing Therapy – which can defuse the distressing memories of trauma and reduce the occurrence of flashbacks, nightmares, and tension. But it is not just a treatment program: for the first time Dr Baker shows what can be done to prevent Post Traumatic Stress. "Knowing how to face trauma," Dr Baker proposes, "and minimize its worst ravages is a skill that we can all benefit from."

Full of first-hand experiences and stories of patients' progress in therapy, this is essential reading for trauma sufferers, their family and friends, and specialists alike.

ISBN: 978-0-7459-5379-3 | £8.99 | $14.95